WAR AND
PRESIDENTIAL
POWER

rightful prerogatives in the area of war powers.

Packed with facts and crystal-clear arguments, *War and Presidential Power* can become the most important book on the subject for this and future generations.

Thomas F. Eagleton is Senator from Missouri. He was a Democratic candidate for Vice President in 1972. He is a graduate of Amherst College and of the Harvard Law School and has served as Attorney General of the State of Missouri. *War and Presidential Power* is his first book.

WAR AND PRESIDENTIAL POWER

A Chronicle of Congressional Surrender

Thomas F. Eagleton

Liveright ▄ New York

LIVERIGHT
386 Park Avenue South
New York, New York 10016

1.987654321

Library of Congress Catalog Card Number: 73-93122
ISBN: 0-87140-581-4

MANUFACTURED IN THE UNITED STATES OF AMERICA

Preface

[I] never expected to hear in a republic a motion
to empower the Executive
alone to declare war.

> ELBRIDGE GERRY
> Constitutional Convention
> Philadelphia
> August 17, 1787

Massachusetts delegate Gerry's indignation at the
motion of Pierce Butler of South Carolina was shared
by his colleagues at the Constitutional Convention.
What, then, might Gerry have said when the Ninety-
third Congress, in 1973, enacted legislation formally
giving away its power to declare war? The United
States had just rid itself of the most unpopular war in
its history, and the American people were ready to
limit sharply the President's warmaking powers.
Congress responded by legitimizing the subservient
role it had mistakenly played during the post-World
War II era.

The new statute, entitled the War Powers Resolution, was, according to its policy section, created "to
fulfill the intent of the framers of the Constitution of
the United States and to insure that the collective
judgment of both the Congress and the President will
apply to the introduction of United States Armed
Forces into hostilities." It does no such thing. Instead, it obliges the President to come to Congress

only *after* American forces have been committed to battle. Up to ninety days of unilateral presidential warmaking is permitted before any specific congressional consent is required. It thus gives legal, albeit unconstitutional, sanction to executive wars in the manner of kingly powers.

I began the following book three years before the current law was enacted. Part I considers the historical evidence for the position I have taken. I had hoped that Part II would be a success story. It became a chronicle of surrender. I had thought that the basic premise of genuine war powers legislation—that Congress alone authorizes war except in specified emergency situations—would survive the legislative process. It did not.

The effort to recapture the war powers of Congress by legislation was inspired by our tragic experience in Indochina. Presidential decisions shaped the course of that war, and an indifferent Congress imposed little or no restraint. So it must have been painfully ironic for Americans to read three weeks after enactment of the War Powers Resolution that the administration was seriously contemplating using the new law as authority to resume bombing in Indochina. Fortunately, Congress had passed a specific restriction against further U.S. combat in that war-torn area, and the administration was forced to concede that the bill could not be used to supercede that restriction. Nevertheless, it was plain to all that Congress had written a blank check for ninety-day presidential wars anywhere else in the world.

Despite the failure of the Ninety-third Congress, I continue to believe that legislation is the only corrective to the current distortion of the Constitution's war clause. I have learned, however, that the good intentions of legislators are far from enough. The American people must understand what is at stake. That is the purpose of this book. Vietnam is the backdrop, but this is not a study of one war. It is an attempt to examine the ways, legal and otherwise, by which our nation goes to war. It is a personal reflection by one whose training is not that of a historian, but that of a lawyer and politician.

I believe the founders were right when they decided to place the responsibility for going to war in the Congress. The imperative to which they held— the avoidance of one-man rule—is even more compelling today. The terrible presidential miscalculations on Vietnam—almost destroying that country while badly dividing our own—argue convincingly for a return to fundamental constitutional principles. We live in a smaller, more dangerous world than did the founders. But rather than diminishing the importance of collective judgment, these changes accentuate that value. The disruption caused by our intervention in Indochina has been amply documented as have been the erroneous assessments of our policy makers. But, in addition, the war brought to the surface long-submerged questions about the effectiveness of the mechanisms within our system for guarding against fallible human judgment. Dependent as it is on the confidence of citizens and on the responsible deliberation of elected representatives, the American system works well only when its interdependent parts are in harmony. The founders understood that when they created three separate but equal branches. And though they may have foreseen temporary fluctuations in the relative power of those branches, the most pessimistic among them could not have anticipated the gradual weakening of one part of the mechanism—the legislative—that would lead to Vietnam and presidential monopoly over the power to make war. Certainly none could have guessed that Congress would one day willingly affirm its own impotence.

It is not possible to say on which day Congress began to lose its power to declare war. Franklin Roosevelt saw a world in peril in 1940, and decided that he would advance the pace of our inevitable involvement in world war, without the prior consent of Congress. But the blame for large-scale institutional erosion is not so easily assigned to one person. I have tried to trace the evolution of the war clause from our beginning as a small agricultural nation, through the era of Manifest Destiny, the trauma of two world wars and into the time of our rise as the dominant nuclear power. A careful review of history shows that, until the modern era, unilateral presidential warmaking was the exception and not the rule. And a close look at the Constitution will show that, by and large, the exceptions were illegal.

An almost continual involvement in war has colored our history. The policies which led to conflict were not always correct, and the individuals who influenced America to go to war, whether in the executive or legislative branches, were certainly not always without fault. Policies and policy makers can be managed by a free society. If they fail, they can be replaced. But an erosion of the constitutional order is a more serious malady and possibly terminal.

I am hopeful that wider awareness of the fundamental law of our land and the history that brought it to life can help reverse the present trend. Whatever one's perspective on American history, the case for sharing the war powers is compelling. The contingencies of a modern era are not sufficient reason to foresake proven wisdom. On the contrary, our will to resist the expedience of one-man decision-making should be reinforced by the events of the past decade. I hope to elucidate that contention in the pages that follow.

Recognitions

Most books have either an acknowledgment or a dedication or both. It seems to me, as a fledgling author, that the more appropriate reference is in the form of a recognition—a recognition of those people who motivated the author and those people who assisted in the preparation of the book.

All of us are products of our environment and upbringing. These people in particular shaped my thought process—my father, Mark Eagleton, a man of boundless energy, imagination, and drive; President Franklin Roosevelt, preeminent politician; President Harry Truman, decisive man of courage and candor; and Eugene Hecker, brilliant teacher and lover of the English language.

A book is not the product of one author alone, but of many patient people who share in its formation. Four people were particularly helpful in this work: Mike and Mary Curzan, a most talented and imaginative couple; Brian Atwood, who skillfully plowed through drafts, redrafts, and re-redrafts; and Carter

Dudley Flemming whose historical research and nimble fingers and toes made the final text reasonably intelligible to the printer.

To all of these, living and dead, I offer my appreciation and the recognition they deserve if the work is judged to have some merit. If it is viewed more negatively, the blame belongs to the author.

Contents

    of War   *184*
12. Surrender   *206*

    Bibliography   *226*
    Index   *233*

Part I

1

Constitutional Principles

The most systematic discussion of the power to make war took place at the Constitutional Convention of 1787. No group has ever thought more deeply about how a free and diverse people ought to be governed than those men who gathered in Philadelphia to write the Constitution of the United States. The delegates were men of learning and high intelligence. They had experienced revolution. They had lived under several different political systems. And they had invested a great deal in the outcome of their deliberations. In the years that have followed, whenever questions have arisen over the proper manner of running a democratic polity, the debates and conclusions of the Founding Fathers have provided a signal point of reference.

These men were doing several things—writing a baptismal certificate for a nation, sanctioning with their reputations a document which espoused some of the most ennobling goals to which any political system could aspire, and setting down rules for the exercise and sharing of power which they hoped would unify a divided people and keep them together. They wrote a statement of the theoretical limitations upon government, of the powers that government was to have and the powers it was not to have. And they spelled out procedures appropriate for the exercise of power.

They had several practical objectives in mind. First, they wished to ensure as much personal freedom as was consistent with order. Second, they hoped to prevent excessive political authority from accumulating in any one institution, for they were all, in varying degrees, skeptical of power. Third, they wanted to impose sufficient restraints on government, so as to prevent it from taking hasty, ill-considered actions.

It is not hard to understand why the writers of the Constitution considered these objectives important; they arose out of common experience. As a matter of philosophy, the Founding Fathers shared the belief of classic British liberalism in certain rights which adhere to the individual and which antedate the establishment of government. Individuals born free, though they may be briefly tyrannized, can be governed only by their own consent. Men will willingly create, and tolerate, only that government which serves their interests. If it does not, it can be overthrown.

The writers of the Constitution lived in a Newtonian age; it was natural for them to search for a rational, balanced, rather mechanistic political structure. Moreover, many of these men shared a vision of human nature as infinitely corruptible, and they were drawn to a formulation of governmental powers that promised to control human weakness by pitting men and institutions against each other. They believed as

Alexander M. Bickel has written of Edmund Burke, that "what mattered was less the source of power than whether it was arbitrary or limited. And the way to prevent power being arbitrary was to ensure that it was nowhere total. A good constitution, therefore, distributed power so that no man or institution held it all, and all who held it balanced and checked one another."

The writers of the Constitution had been raised as Englishmen, inside a colonial empire. They were accustomed to a strong executive authority that assured an ordered society which adapted slowly to changing conditions. On the other hand, their experience had fostered a deep distrust of inordinate executive power, as they felt that power being exercised by colonial governors and by the English king. Dissatisfied with what they considered arbitrary rule, the Founding Fathers waged a war for independence—but thereafter, the ultimate implications of what this had done began to distress them. They understood that freedom and authority were not antagonists but inseparable companions. The disorder of government under the Articles of Confederation and the concomitant domestic upheavals pointed to the need for a stronger federal government; yet they were not eager to submit the new nation, and themselves, to an all-powerful central authority. In short, they wisely accommodated their hopes to their fears, agreeing that while there were virtues in executive power and virtues in legislative power, there were great hazards in permitting any one authority to become dominant.

The plan they adopted called for dividing power between three branches—executive, legislative, and judicial—each branch designed to check the others. They concluded, as Jefferson wrote in his autobiog-

raphy, that "it is not by the consolidation, or concentration of powers, but by their distribution that
good government is effected."

But in apportioning power, the Constitution gave
the Congress the preeminent position, because it
most nearly represented, even before universal suf-
frage, the people. It was the body most likely to reflect *all* opinions, argue *all* options, and to raise objections to any suggested course of action. In the end,
whatever the suspicions and hostilities of the framers
toward "the people," they feared unrepresentative
and arbitrary authority more. Even Alexander Hamilton, hardly a populist, conceded in his defense of the
Constitution "the superior weight and influence of
the legislative body in a free government."

Congress was given not only a long and full list of
powers, but the residual authority

> To make all Laws which shall be necessary and
> proper for carrying into Execution the foregoing Pow-
> ers, and all other powers vested by this Constitution
> in the Government of the United States, or in any
> Department or Office thereof.

The inclusion in the Constitution of this clause
raised the possibility that the legislature might arrogate to itself vast powers, perhaps even usurping the
authority of the other branches of government. The
founders perceived this danger, but reluctantly accepted it as the lesser of several evils. James Madison concluded that if Congress should be "without
the *substance* of this [residual] power, the whole
Constitution would be a dead letter."

This does not mean that these scholarly draftsmen
did nothing to guard against intemperate legislators.
On the contrary, the executive branch was to be a

counterweight. Concerned about "the tendency of the legislative authority to absorb every other," Hamilton led the forces of those who stressed the need for an independently elected chief executive who would be strong enough to prevent a "popular" tyranny.

But how could they create a strong executive, one who could check a reckless legislature, without risking a capricious executive? In the end, the powers of the executive branch were defined less clearly than those of the legislature. Hamilton, in a somewhat extreme statement, wrote that the executive shall be "limited to executive details" in the administration of government. He went on to state:

> The actual conduct of foreign negotiation, the preparatory plans of finance, the application and disbursement of public moneys in conformity to the general appropriations of the legislature, the arrangement of the army and navy, the direction of the operations of war—these, and other matters of like nature, constitute what seems to be most properly understood by the administration of government.

It is generally agreed, however, that the founders did not mean to circumscribe the chief executive as sharply as Hamilton suggested. Rather than stripping the executive branch of all discretion, the Constitution positions the discretionary powers of the President and his subordinates within rather narrow guidelines that are subject to legislative scrutiny.

The framers were aware that by giving both specific and residual powers to the Congress and a somewhat undefined charter to the President, they had fashioned a system of concurrent authority. And they had little doubt that by doing so, they had sowed the seeds for possible conflict. How this conflict—if it occurred—should be resolved was reasonably clear to them. Compromise would be sought at almost any cost, but if negotiations proved fruitless, overriding control would remain with the Congress. If the conflict centered on an action already begun, the Congress would not be forced to accept a *fait accompli*. Again, it was Hamilton who wrote:

> The legislature is still free to perform its duties, according to its own sense of them; though the executive, in the exercise of its constitutional powers, may establish an antecedent state of things, which ought to weigh in the legislative decisions.

In short, a Congress moving to reverse the policies of a President must step warily. Nevertheless, it could not ultimately be forbidden the right to circumscribe antecedent presidential action.

Nowhere in the Constitution did the framers make more of an effort to force the legislative and executive branches to share responsibility for policy making than in the provisions which deal with the power to make war. In those sections they strove to set up a procedure under which neither branch of the federal government could make war without the aid of the other—a procedure which would strike a delicate balance between legislative primacy and executive efficiency.

Most issues are dealt with by the Constitution through one reference. The waging of war and the responsibility for military forces are treated at various places. Thus:

—Article I, Section 8, gives the Congress power to "declare War," grant "Letters of Marque," order "Reprisal," "raise and support Armies"—for no more than two years at a time—"provide and maintain a Navy," make rules which will regulate and govern the military forces, and provide for organizing the militia and calling it up so that insurrections can be suppressed and invasions repelled.

—Article I, Section 10, forbids the states—without congressional consent—from keeping military forces in time of peace and from engaging "in war, unless actually invaded, or in such imminent Danger as will not admit of delay."

—Article II, Section 2, makes the President "Commander in Chief of the Army and Navy of the United States, and of the Militia of the several States, when called into the actual service of the United States."

—Article IV, Section 4, provides that the central government shall guarantee "a Republican Form of Government" to every state and "shall protect each of them against Invasion."

These provisions of the Constitution were not devised to provide exact answers to every question that might arise regarding the use of American troops or the appropriate responses to acts of hostility or war by foreign nations. They were devised so that the Congress, the chief executive, and the states would have a framework within which they could cooperate in the protection of the nation from external harm. Going to war was intended to be an orderly process in which deliberation would be given full play before conflict began and in which reason and caution would be used once hostilities had commenced. It was the hope that every effort would be made to prevent war through chance or mistake and that prudence and countervailing power would strengthen the forces of rationality. The scheme for ensuring these aims was relatively simple.

First, the founders drew a crucial distinction between offensive and defensive hostilities. If the United States were attacked, the commander in chief would repel the attack. If an individual state was militarily challenged—even it would possess a right to fight back. Thus, the states could maintain militia which would be available for duty if hostilities arose. For on its part, Congress could provide the President with a small standing army and navy so that he could fulfill his duty to put down insurrection, although such a course was frowned upon. In addition, Congress was authorized to establish procedures under which the President might nationalize state militia rapidly, so that he might respond effectively to foreign attack.

Second, in cases where defensive action needed to be supplemented or replaced by offensive action, the concurrence of Congress would be required. There was little concern that time might be lost in the process. To the framers, the judgment of the entire nation, acting through its elected representatives, would have to be sought once the issue was no longer that of repelling attacking forces. Thus, whether simple reprisals or complex military operations or all-out war were involved, the Congress was to sanction these actions before they started.

Third, the President would direct military operations: Congress would play no part in the day-to-day tactics. This decision of the draftsmen of the Constitution was made clear when they decided to change the term "make war"—which might imply the concept of Congress conducting hostilities and which had been in an earlier draft of the document—to "declare war," which carried with it the connotation of Congress initiating hostilities.

Concomitantly, the role of the President as commander in chief was clarified by both the delegates to the Constitutional Convention and by Madison, Hamilton, and Jay, authors of *The Federalist Papers*. Their records make clear that surprise was shown at the convention when the possibility was raised of giving the President power to make decisions which might lead to military offensives. As delegate Gerry commented, he "never expected to hear in a republic, a motion to empower the Executive alone to declare war." It should be added that *no* such motion ever carried. As Hamilton noted in a slightly different context:

> The history of human conduct does not warrant that exalted opinion of human virtue which would make it wise in a nation to commit interests of so delicate and momentous a kind, as those which concern its intercourse with the rest of the world, to the sole disposal of a magistrate created and circumstances as would be a President of the United States.

Thus, it would appear that the title of commander in chief did not carry with it war-initiating authority. In the words of *The Federalist Papers*, the role of commander in chief

> would amount to nothing more than the supreme command and direction of the military and naval forces, as first General and admiral of the Confederacy; while that of the British king extends to the *declaring* of war and to the *raising* and *regulating* of fleets and armies,—all which, by the Constitution under consideration, would appertain to the legislature.

It must be stressed that this statement was addressed to the basic question of the President as *policy maker* on matters of war or peace. When Hamilton later turned his attention to the commander in chief's tactical powers, he set forth a far different position. Once hostilities had begun, the President was to have wide discretion. For once war had been declared

> the direction of . . . [it] most peculiarly demands those qualities which distinguish the exercise of power by a single hand. The direction of war implies the direction of the common strength; and the power of directing and employing the common strength, forms a usual and essential part in the definition of the executive authority.

Fourth, the start of hostilities was not to mark the end of congressional responsibility. For while Congress was not to make particular, tactical decisions, it would not surrender its wider policy prerogatives. At the least, the changeover from defensive to offensive action would have to be sanctioned by the legislature. Similarly, decisions resulting in major changes in tactics—changes which might bring new opponents into a war, for example—would be an appropriate subject for congressional concern. At the same time, the Founding Fathers were realistic enough to anticipate that a strong-willed President exercising his power as commander in chief, might be very reluctant to return to Congress for approval, or even counsel, once hostilities had begun. In effect, powerful Presidents would naturally equate tactical decisions with policy decisions. The response of the Founding Fathers to this dilemma was to give the Congress full power over the expenditure of funds for the military and to insist that the Congress review military appropriations at least every two years. According to *The Federalist Papers:*

> The whole power of raising armies was lodged in the Legislature . . . [subject to] an important qualification . . . which forbids the appropriation of money for the support of an army for any longer period than two years—a precaution which, upon a nearer view of it, will appear to be a great and real security against the keeping of troops without evident necessity.

It thus appears that the framers of the Constitution, having debated every contingency they could imagine, faced the possibility that Congress might someday be forced to deal with a strong and militant President whose course it might wish to deflect. They dealt with that possibility by giving Congress enough power to check a President whose military objectives went beyond or were contrary to those of the legislative branch.

These sections of the Constitution, like all of its other dictates, were the bare bones of our national beginning, requiring the flesh of historical experience. The life and meaning of the charter would evolve from events and human reactions to them. Interpretations of a few short phrases, describing the way in which the United States could undertake hostilities, began to be made almost immediately as Congresses and Presidents sought to delineate their respective rights. The debate has stretched across almost two centuries of major and minor wars, incursions, reprisals, and police actions.

2

The Early Experience:
Draftsmen as Statesmen

The administrations of George Washington, John Adams, Thomas Jefferson, James Madison, and James Monroe were peopled largely by those who had been present at the Constitutional Convention in Philadelphia or had taken an active part in the politics of ratifying the Constitution. Precedents established in these early years can, therefore, be properly viewed as accurate indices of the intentions of the framers.

It must be noted that the early interpretations of the Constitution's meanings were partially conditioned by the founders' knowledge of English law and custom. Certainly this was true with regard to the war powers provisions. It was Alexander Hamilton who noted in Federalist Paper 26 that Americans derived their ideas about the control of the military "from the nation from whom the inhabitants of these states have in general sprung."

By 1789, in England, Parliament had become the

dominant force in military affairs; indeed it had been
so since the early seventeenth century. No king had
been able to wage war without parliamentary consent
since 1626.* The monarch could not put into effect a
treaty without Parliament's giving its advice and
consent. Only Parliament had the right to raise and
maintain a standing army. It was Parliament that
granted and removed military commissions. Even
command of the troops had been shifted from the
monarch to the cabinet during the early years of the
eighteenth century. At the beginning of the War of
the Spanish Succession, when Queen Anne ascended
to the throne in 1702, command of the troops was
transferred from the queen to Lord Marlborough as
captain general. Marlborough made this office a powerful one, and as a member of the cabinet—which
had become the effective executive presence between 1689 and 1714—he brought the prestige of the
captain general into that body. Thereafter, the power
of command passed to the cabinet itself.

Early interpretations of the war powers provisions
of the U.S. Constitution, conditioned by these English precedents, were also influenced by the military experience during the American Revolution.
As commander in chief, Washington had respected
legislative supremacy; he served under a commission
granted him by the Continental Congress in June
1775 and returned by him to the Congress in December 1783. The final paragraph of that commission
read:

* In 1626, when Charles I tried to make war without parliamentary consent, Parliament voted him no money. The impossibility of continuing
the war without parliamentary financing led Charles to sign the Petition
of Right (1628), which declared it illegal to collect any taxes without parliamentary consent, thus ending forever the possibility of the king's waging war without parliamentary authorization.

And you are to regulate your conduct in every respect by the rules and disciplines of war (as herewith given you) and punctually to observe and follow such orders and directions from time to time as you shall receive from this or a future Congress of the said United Colonies or a committee of Congress for that purpose appointed.

The Articles of Confederation likewise embodied the principle of legislative supremacy. Article IX of that document stated, "The united states in Congress assembled, shall have the sole and exclusive right and power of determining on peace and war. . . ."

The national government's first trial by arms came in 1798—against its oldest and closest ally, France. By then, the ruling Directory in Paris and the Federalist administration of John Adams had accumulated a number of mutual misunderstandings. The French had condemned Adams for his "pro-British" foreign policy. In turn, the Federalists had been irritated by the actions of the French government's representatives in actively supporting their political rivals, Jefferson's Republicans, in the election of 1796.

These antagonisms came to a head when in 1798, during a naval war between France and Britain, the French government authorized its ships to seize and confiscate all American vessels bound to or from British ports or engaged in carrying British goods. Although U.S. shipping was harassed, President Adams took no independent action to protect the nation's commerce. Instead, he waited for the Congress to pass statutes authorizing military action and suspending commercial relations with France. In a special message to Congress on May 16, 1797, Adams said: "It remains for Congress to prescribe such regulations as will enable our seafaring citizens to defend themselves against violations of the law of nations, and at the same time, restrain them from committing acts of hostility against the powers of war." The Congress thereupon authorized certain steps against the French. While refraining from a formal declaration of war, it originated and broadly defined what it considered an appropriate response to a hostile foreign power.

In the two years of naval warfare between France and the United States, France lost more than eighty vessels. In the best-known naval battles, the U.S.S. *Constellation* defeated *L'Insurgente* and the *Vengeance*. Americans were elated, and their pride undiminished by the knowledge that the French navy was simultaneously fighting both the British and the Americans on the high seas. President Adams, however, was less than ardent over the naval war with France and in 1799 sent a commission to Paris, which in 1800 successfully concluded negotiations with Napoleon.

Peace had returned to the country, but unfortunately the country was not yet ready for that peace. The public turned upon Adams and his party and voted them out of office. Nevertheless, Adams never lost confidence in the correctness of the steps he had taken to prevent the fledgling nation from being dragged into a major war. Fifteen years after he had been defeated for a second term as President, he wrote:

> I will defend my missions to France, as long as I have an eye to direct my hand, or a finger to hold my pen. They were the most disinterested and meritorious actions of my life. I reflect upon them with so much satisfaction, that I desire no other inscription over my gravestone than: "Here lies John Adams, who took

upon himself the responsibility of peace with France in the year 1800."

Interestingly enough, the battle with France produced not only executive and legislative interpretations of the war powers provisions, but the first judicial interpretations of those provisions as well. In *Bas* v. *Tingy,* the Supreme Court was asked to decide whether the United States was at war at the time that an American ship was rescued from the French. It ruled that Congress had placed the United States at war—even though the authorized hostilities were confined to naval action. The proposition set forth was that Congress was not limited to formal declarations by its power to initiate hostilities; it could authorize, and thereby control, military actions that fell short of total war between two nations. In reaching this decision, Justice Washington wrote that Congress could unquestionably declare a war "of the perfect kind, because one whole nation is at war with another whole nation, and all the members of the nation declaring war, are authorized to commit hostilities against all the members of the other, in every place, and under every circumstance." But the justice added that there were also wars "of the imperfect kind, more properly called acts of hostility, or reprisal" characterized by being "more confined in . . . nature and extent; being limited as to places, persons, and things." These also were public wars, because they were "an external contention by force between some of the members of the two nations, authorized by Congress." * Justice Chase, concurring, noted that

* Wars were as unlikely to be declared formally in the eighteenth century as they are in the twentieth. Alexander Hamilton noted in *The Federalist Papers* that declarations of war had fallen into disuse. Justice

Congress had taken the permissible route of declaring "hostilities . . . by certain persons in certain cases." He went on to state that for Congress to so act "only proves the circumspection and prudence of the legislature." Finally, Justice Paterson supported this unanimous sanctioning of the power of Congress to declare wars limited in time or scope or area:

> As far as Congress tolerated and authorized the war on our part, so far may we proceed in hostile operations. . . . It is therefore a public war between the two nations qualified, on our part, in the manner prescribed by the constitutional organ of our country.

The *Bas* case was the first judicial interpretation of the range of congressional powers to declare and to circumscribe hostilities. In turn, *Talbot* v. *Seeman*, represents the first judicial determination of which branch of government must bear responsibility for taking the nation into either full-scale or limited hostilities. In *Talbot*, it was newly appointed Chief Justice John Marshall who, in deciding the status of a German ship seized by the French for their use and then taken by American naval forces, wrote:

> The whole powers of war being, by the constitution of the United States vested in Congress, the *acts of that body can alone* be resorted to as our guides in this inquiry. It is not denied, nor in the course of the argu-

---

Story, in his *Commentaries on the Constitution*, made the same assertion. Of the 117 wars which took place throughout the world between 1700 and 1870, only 10 were declared. Thus, it may be inferred that the Founding Fathers expected "perfect wars to be the exception, rather than the rule." It follows that in giving Congress power to declare war, they had no intention of limiting Congress and removing it from the decision-making process in the majority of war situations. They meant rather, as the *Bas* case clearly indicates, to include all military actions under the term "war."

ment has it been denied, that *congress may authorize general hostilities,* in which case the general laws of war, so far as they actually apply to our situation, must be noticed.

Three years later, Marshall had a further opportunity to expound upon the relative powers of the executive branch and the Congress. In *Little* v. *Barreme,* the issue before the Court again involved the legality of a ship seizure during U.S.-French naval hostilities. The dispute arose from the fact that in 1799 Congress had authorized the seizure of American ships bound *for* French ports. In this instance, the vessel which had been taken was en route *from* a French port to the Danish island of St. Thomas. In a short opinion, Marshall held that the seizure was in conflict with the congressional will and therefore illegal. In reaching this decision, the chief justice stressed that if Congress had simply declared a naval war against the French, the President, "as commander in chief of the armies and navies . . . might . . . without any special authority for that purpose," have had power to seize an American ship bound from France. But Congress had not done this; it had stated that American ships *bound to* France could be seized. By doing so, it had effectively preempted presidential discretion and "prescribed that the manner in which this law shall be carried into execution . . . excludes a seizure of any vessel not bound to a French port."

Through these three early decisions, the Supreme Court laid the foundation for later interpretations of the warmaking powers. To the Court, "the whole powers" of entering into an offensive war were vested in the Congress "alone." Included in these powers was authority to declare either general or narrowly limited hostilities. Presidential authority to take offensive action under the guise of his power as commander in chief arose only *after* Congress had acted. Moreover, while the tactics of warfare might require that the President have certain discretionary powers, even these could be narrowed by precedent legislative action.

The Supreme Court did not stand alone. As early as 1789, Thomas Jefferson wrote Madison: "We have already given, in example, one effectual check to the dog of war, by transferring the power of declaring war from the executive to the legislative body, from those who are to spend, to those who are to pay." In 1793, Jefferson, then secretary of state, wrote that if the United States should ever decide to take "reprisal on a nation . . . Congress must be called upon to take it; the right of reprisal being expressly lodged with them by the Constitution, and not with the Executive." Twelve years later, President Jefferson— whom historians have classified as a strong chief executive—sent a message to Congress with reference to a dispute between the United States and Tripoli, in which he noted that "Congress alone is constitutionally invested with the power of changing our condition from peace to war."

Presidents James Madison and James Monroe followed these Jeffersonian guidelines. During the administration of President Madison, Congress passed its first formal declaration of war, sanctioning the War of 1812. The background is revealing for it illustrates the deference, at that time, of the executive to the will of the Congress.

Throughout the monumental struggle of the early 1800s—known as the Napoleonic wars—American shipping and American seamen were harassed by both France and Great Britain. By 1810, the United States had ample justification to declare war against either nation, although it lacked both the military manpower and the financial resources for such a confrontation. Nevertheless, in the second decade of the century, a coalition of forces began to push us toward war with Great Britain. Several factors came into play. Among these were the British government's unwillingness to amend its policy of violating free American shipping, the French government's success in fanning American hostility toward British policy, and a growing desire of the northwestern sections of the United States to remove British influence from Canada.

The forces for war were overwhelmingly western and southern. One of the leading spokesmen for the War Hawks—the term given the western advocates of war in Congress—was Henry Clay, and a statement he made in 1810 is representative of that position:

> No man in the nation wants peace more than I, but I prefer the troubled ocean of war, demanded by the honor and independence of this country, with all its calamities and desolation [sic], to the tranquil and putrescent pool of ignominious peace. If we can accommodate our differences with one of the belligerents only, I should prefer that one to be Britain; but if with neither, and we are forced into a selection of our enemy, then I am for war with Britain, because I believe her prior in aggression, and her injuries and insults to us more atrocious in character. . . . It is said, however, that no object is obtainable by war with Great Britain. In its fortunes we are to estimate not only the benefit to be derived to ourselves, but the injury to . . . the enemy.

However, war with Great Britain was opposed by the New England states, whose commercial interests would be endangered by conflict. To the cold and stern Federalist businessmen, France was more to be feared than Great Britain. War with England would only serve to depress American commerce further. Indeed, not even the long sought-after annexation of western lands held any interest to the men of New England. To them, new states would support Jefferson, strengthening the Republican party and not the Federalists.

Eventually, however, the pressures for hostilities became irresistible, and on June 1, 1812, President Madison asked Congress for a declaration of war, stating that he did so because warmaking was a "solemn question which the Constitution wisely confides to the legislative department of the Government." The measure passed the House of Representatives by 79 to 49 and the Senate by 19 to 13.

Between June 1, 1812, and the fall election, the British government ended the most objectionable of its interference with American commerce, and the possibility of a peaceful settlement of the shipping question emerged. The election of 1812 became, therefore, a referendum on the war question. The Federalist candidate, DeWitt Clinton of New York was the peace candidate. Madison was firmly committed to the War Hawks, and his 1812 victory is attributable to western and southern support. From a geographical standpoint, the popular vote in 1812 almost exactly paralleled the congressional decision on the declaration of war. The nation had told its leaders that victory, not compromise, was desired.

Just as President Madison adhered strictly to the

language of the Constitution in taking the country into the War of 1812, President Monroe carefully construed constitutional language in his conduct of the Seminole War. This war, which occurred in 1818, brought forth the first presidential claim of a constitutional power to defend U.S. territory. It arose from attacks by the Seminole Indian tribe from its base in Florida—then owned by Spain—on settlements in the United States. After attacking, the Indians retreated across the border. In a message to Congress on March 25, 1818, President Monroe assured the legislature that any military action he might take would be kept within constitutional bounds. He then went on to justify his authority to defend American citizens by noting that Spain was bound by a treaty of 1795 to restrain the Indians within Florida's borders from attacking the territory of the United States. He stated that Spain had not fulfilled this obligation, and, in fact, had insufficient troops in Florida to do so. As a result, the U.S. Army would have to undertake what Spain had not done, lest American citizens be endangered by Spain's failure to keep its commitments. Nevertheless, President Monroe was scrupulous in asserting the right only of self-defense; he noted that "orders have been given to the general in command not to enter Florida unless it be in pursuit of the enemy."

President Monroe was likewise faithful to Jeffersonian thinking when he issued the Monroe Doctrine in 1824. In setting forth this country's protective role in Latin America, Monroe and Secretary of State John Quincy Adams did not alter the constitutional balance in regard to the question of warmaking. In responding to requests for assistance from Latin American countries, Monroe stated that "the Executive has no right to compromit the nation in any question of war." Secretary Adams added that should an attack be launched by a nation in Europe on a South American republic, the Monroe administration's position would be that "the power to determine our resistance is in Congress."

It is often said that during this formative period in our history, one voice, that of Alexander Hamilton, spoke for broader Presidential authority. In support of this theory, reliance is placed on Hamilton's writings during 1801–5, when this country engaged in hostilities against Tripoli. The facts do not seem to support the claim. During the early years of the Republic, American shipping in the Mediterranean and eastern Atlantic was preyed upon by the warships of the Barbary States of northwest Africa. To protect its commerce, the United States made treaties with and paid tribute to the states, Algiers, Tripoli, Tunis, and Morocco. But in 1801, the pasha of Tripoli, convinced that he was not getting his fair share of the payments, ordered the flag cut down from the U.S. consulate—a provocative hint that more hostile actions might follow. Jefferson thereupon stationed a squadron of American warships near Gibraltar; Tripoli declared war and attacked the ships, and under orders from Jefferson, the American fleet disarmed the attackers, then let them go. It was Jefferson's opinion that he was "unauthorized by the Constitution" and "without the sanction of Congress to go beyond the line of defense" in dealing with these attacks. He then requested "authorizing measures of offense," which Congress quickly granted.

Jefferson's restraint enraged Hamilton. In structuring his attack on the President, however, Hamilton took care to make it consistent with generally accepted principles. He wrote:

> "The Congress shall have power to declare war;" the plain meaning of which is, that it is the peculiar and exclusive province of Congress, *when the nation is at peace*, to change that state into a state of war; whether from calculations of policy, or from provocations or injuries received; in other words, it belongs to Congress only, *to go to war*.

But to Hamilton, the Tripoli situation did not fall within these guidelines, for Tripoli had declared war on the United States by proclamation and by deed. Under these conditions, he believed, the Constitution gave the President power to respond on his own; the President, he said, surely could at least eliminate the military forces that were attacking U.S. forces. Hamilton's position in this instance cannot reasonably be read as a brief for the right of a President to initiate hostilities. He asked only that the President interpret his right to repel attacks on American military forces as meaning that he could act to eliminate the military threat which the enemy posed, even before Congress formally gave its assent.

Now two hundred years later, the war powers provisions of the Constitution are often interpreted in ways that are radically at variance with the original concept of the Founding Fathers. To understand this, we must first examine the circumstances under which the original interpretations were modified and the extent of those modifications; and second, determine if the changes have been helpful or harmful to the nation.

3

The Nineteenth Century

Legal scholars of the nineteenth century held that extensive consultation required by the Constitution on the making of war served several ends. One, of course, was the preservation of a basic principle: that the people and their representatives would make the major decisions affecting their lives and property. As Justice Joseph Story wrote in 1833: "The representatives of the people are to lay the taxes to support a war, and therefore have a right to be consulted, as to its propriety and necessity. The executive is to carry it on, and therefore should be consulted, as to its time, and the ways and means of making it effective." It was accepted dogma that this consultation, in and of itself, had the desired end of discouraging military adventurism. "It should," Justice Story said, "be difficult in a republic to declare war; but not to make peace."

Story's thoughts paralleled those of the Founding Fathers. The single most striking feature of the nineteenth-century politicians' concept and use of war powers was the degree to which these men held to the theories and practices of their predecessors. In approving broad legislative authorizations permitting Presidents to operate against pirate bands in the Mediterranean, the Caribbean, or the Pacific, Congress defined concrete infringements of American rights; it then gave the President authority to act in those instances. Thus, in March 1815, Congress sanctioned the use of armed vessels "as may be judged requisite by the President" to protect American commerce in the Atlantic and the Mediterranean. This act which, among other things, made it lawful to take prizes, led to the Second Barbary War. A similar congressional act took effect in 1822 and authorized military strikes against privateers operating in the Caribbean, particularly out of ports in Cuba and Puerto Rico.

This procedure under which congressional authorization preceded presidential action was not only followed when small nations and pirate chieftains were the present or potential foe. Congress was consulted and asked for permissive legislation when the adversary was large and powerful. During the late 1830s, when disagreement arose between the United States and Great Britain over Canada's border, President Martin Van Buren made certain that his actions had congressional sanction. War was averted; nevertheless, having obtained congressional authority and funds, Van Buren was prepared to fight the British if necessary.

The primacy of Congress was demonstrated in the early 1840s when popular pressure mounted to send U.S. military forces to intervene in a dispute between France and the kingdom of Hawaii. Daniel Webster was secretary of state and he was not to be panicked. "The war-making power in this Government," he wrote, "rests entirely with Congress. . . . The President . . . [could] authorize belligerent operations only in the cases expressly provided for by the Constitution and the laws."

The force of Jeffersonian precedents was again shown in 1859, when President James Buchanan sought authority from the Congress to respond to attacks on American ships and U.S. citizens by various Latin American governments. The language of Buchanan's request was familiar:

> The executive government of this country in its intercourse with foreign nations is limited to the employment of diplomacy alone. When this fails it can proceed no further. It can not legitimately resort to force without the direct authority of Congress, except in resisting and repelling hostile attacks.

President Andrew Johnson, criticized by the Congress and nearly impeached for allegedly overstepping the proper bounds of prerogatives never asserted his exclusive right to make war. In his one major military venture—a threat of force against the French in Mexico—Johnson conferred with the legislators and scrupulously kept them informed of all measures he was taking, their risks and their probable consequences. Johnson never went beyond sending troops to the Mexican border and dispatching sharp notes to the French commander in Mexico. By 1866 his demands for French withdrawals had been met. Some twenty-five thousand French troops left Mexico.

These examples of presidential awareness of the rights and duties of Congress can be matched by instances of congressional protection of its constitutional mandate. In 1869, President Grant signed a

treaty with the Dominican Republic under which
that country would be annexed to the United States.
While the treaty was being considered by the U.S.
Senate, Grant authorized the American navy to protect the Dominican Republic from an attack by Haiti.
Senate disapproval of Grant's act was prompt. Numerous senators rose in protest during the floor debates of March 1871, the most outspoken being Senator Charles Sumner of Massachusetts, dean of the
Senate. Sumner introduced several resolutions calling for withdrawal of the American naval presence
from the Dominican Republic and rejecting Grant's
right to order such action in the first place. On March
27, 1871, Sumner spoke on the floor of the Senate for
four and a half hours, arguing in his opening statement that "on evidence now before the Senate, it is
plain that the Navy of the United States, acting under
orders from Washington, has been engaged in measures of violence and of belligerent intervention,
being war, without the authority of Congress."

President Grant had his defenders. Some like Senator Frederick Theodore Frelinghuysen of New Jersey roundly condemned Sumner for criticizing Grant.
In Frelinghuysen's emotional words:

> I said the Senator had denounced the deliverer of
> my country, and has he not? Where is the warm-
> hearted lover of his country who does not feel that
> General Grant, as the instrument of God, brought us
> deliverance? He saved my hearth-stone from desola-
> tion, he has perpetuated to my children an inheritance
> more precious than any that I hope to leave them.
> From the inmost recesses of an honest heart I am
> grateful to him and honor him. Yes, and in thousands
> and tens of thousands of homes at the North and West
> and East, where the father still grieves that his son has

gone from him forever, where the young wife still wears the weeds of sorrow, where the mother hears in the sighing of the trees the death-cry of her boy this reverence and love for the name of the nation's deliverer is a living passion.

Turning more directly to the matter at issue, Frelinghuysen insisted that Grant had not exceeded his constitutional powers. "The power," he said, "is inherent in his office. He is the head and the Executive of the nation. . . . Our President cannot declare war; but if while he is discharging his constitutional duty of taking care of the nation's dignity or interests war results from his action, it is a lawful war." That argument, too, was to be heard again many years later. But it was not then the prevailing argument.

Perhaps the best exposition of the constitutional question that Grant's action posed was presented on the Senate floor by Senator Carl Schurz of Missouri. Schurz noted that the President had not ordered the military forces of the United States to engage in military acts, except under certain contingencies and to protect American interests. "But," the senator asked, "has the President the power under the Constitution at his own arbitrary pleasure and discretion to define a contingency in which the arms of the United States shall be used against a nation with whom the United States are at peace? Has he the unlimited discretionary power to order the use of arms in a contingency so defined by himself?" Might the President, Schurz wondered, conclude a treaty with a foreign nation, under the terms of which he could undertake military action which could not normally be undertaken unilaterally under the Constitution? The senator was fearful that "the President, of whom nobody pretends that he possesses the power to initiate a war of his own motion under the Constitution, still does possess, the power, by making a treaty, to create an inchoate right of the United States in some foreign territory, and having by his own arbitrary act created that inchoate right, he has the power at his arbitrary pleasure, without authority from Congress, to commit acts of war for the enforcement of that inchoate right."

In the end, the Senate showed its disapproval—not by passing resolutions condemning the President, but by defeating Grant's proposed treaty with the Dominican Republic. The President thereupon rescinded his naval orders, prior to the outbreak of any hostilities.

Five years later, Grant maneuvered more discreetly when he concluded that force might be necessary to restore order in Cuba. He informed the Congress of the situation and stated, "In view of the gravity of this question, I have deemed it my duty to invite the attention of the war-making power of the country to all the relations and bearings of the question." After reviewing in some detail the situation in Cuba, Grant ended by saying that if a response should appear necessary, he would recommend to the Congress "what may then seem to me to be necessary."

In summary, nineteenth-century Presidents more often than not conscientiously respected the Constitution's delineation of the war powers. Two final examples of presidential statements can be cited. The first is that of President Chester A. Arthur in his second annual message to the Congress in 1882:

A recent agreement with Mexico provides for the crossing of the frontier by the armed forces of either country in pursuit of hostile Indians. In my message of last year I called attention to the prevalent lawlessness upon the border and to the necessity of legislation for its suppression. I again invite the attention of Congress to the subject.

The second example is from President Benjamin Harrison's message to Congress in 1891, reviewing the history of an incident concerning two American sailors on shore leave in Chile who had been physically attacked, and the President's attempts to negotiate satisfactory compensation. He concluded: "If these just expectations should be disappointed or further needless delay intervene, I will by a special message bring this matter again to the attention of Congress for such action as may be necessary."

Admittedly, there were exceptions to this pattern of congressional-executive coresponsibility. One grew out of the imperative of protecting American citizens and their property abroad. In an era when communications were slow and uncertain, Presidents were obliged to give their naval commanders broad powers to intervene in foreign lands to protect American lives. Over time, and long after communication had become speedier and more reliable, this responsibility came to be viewed as a legitimate extension of the presidential power of self-defense. Similarly, Presidents gradually began to give their naval commanders broader discretion to retaliate against pirates or others who interfered with American shipping. The unwritten assumption was that such actions should be taken only against persons who were not subject to any other constituted governmental authority, or against countries too weak and too primitive to engage the United States inadvertently in a costly war. So long as this was understood,

Congress and the President accepted the proposition that such military acts could be engaged in without specific congressional consent. And indeed they were, from approximately the third decade of the nineteenth century onward.

The only serious congressional question ever raised over a protective or retaliatory action came in 1854 during the administration of President Franklin Pierce. That year, an American naval vessel bombarded Greytown, Nicaragua. The shelling occurred after the American minister to Central America was slightly injured during a domestic upheaval in that city—the upshot of a dispute between two rival commercial groups set up to transport travelers across the Isthmus of Panama. The naval officer in command of the U.S.S. *Cyane*, which was stationed nearby, acted under rather vague instructions issued by the secretary of the navy regarding the protection of American citizens. Congress had not authorized any use of military force against Nicaragua, but the officer took it upon himself to revenge the insult to an American diplomat. When the news reached the United States, President Pierce defended the officer but not without some embarrassment. According to most accounts of the period, Pierce's defense appears to have derived from his view of his role as chief administrative officer of the government responsible for the deeds of his subordinates, rather than on his right as commander in chief to authorize on his own any act of war.

Pierce's position was perhaps best expressed later in the year after Cuba had seized an American vessel. The President reported to Congress that he was seeking an "amicable adjustment" but that if negotiations failed, he would "not hesitate to use the authority and means *which Congress may grant* to insure the observance of our just rights. . . ."

During present-day debate over this question, the behavior of Abraham Lincoln at the start of the Civil War has been cited as precedent. But the analogy is strained. Lincoln claimed exclusive powers to repel attacks or insurrections which clearly threatened the survival of the Union. But as to presidential power to take offensive military actions against foreign countries in order to prevent threats to, or limit attacks upon, American citizens or property—his views were in line with the classic position of the Founding Fathers. The Constitution was framed, Lincoln wrote, so "that no one man should hold the power of bringing oppressions upon us"; it did not allow any President "to make war at his pleasure." The Civil War did not begin at the "pleasure of the President." It was a struggle, as Lincoln saw it, forced upon the federal government, and he had no doubt that the nation must remain one. Nor, when secession occurred and was followed by an attack on Fort Sumter, was the Congress in doubt. The President took strong countermeasures, among which was an order blockading various Southern ports. Thereafter, Lincoln sought congressional ratification for his actions— which was quickly given. During the period following the proclamation of the blockade but prior to congressional ratification of it, however, several Southern ships were seized. The legality of the seizure was challenged and this challenge raised the issue of the validity of the presidentially imposed blockade. For the first time since the early 1800s, the question of warmaking returned to the federal courts.

The Supreme Court, in the *Prize Cases*, split 5 to 4,

the majority opinion reflecting a position that might well have been argued by Alexander Hamilton, the minority reflecting a Jeffersonian outlook. Considering the weight which advocates of broad presidential war powers have given this case, it is interesting to observe that the majority kept its holding in close context, asserting that no major changes in constitutional theory were being advanced. To the majority, the President had "no power to initiate or declare a war either against a foreign nation or a domestic State." But once war had been declared on the United States, the President had to determine "the shape" of the conflict and decide upon the "degree of force the crisis demand[ed]." This was no blank check to the executive to respond militarily in ways wholly disproportionate to the danger; nor did the majority of the Court mean that *ex post facto* congressional ratification should not be sought. The decision meant that *when the nation's political integrity was militarily challenged,* the President had the power to order at least a blockade of the attackers' ports. Thus, the *Prize Cases* may be seen as a clarification of the President's powers under the constitutional right of self-defense. The holding in the case did not, however, represent a departure from established doctrines and practices.

One series of episodes during the nineteenth century did seem to violate earlier precedents. They centered on Texas and its admission to the Union and marked the first important dispute in our history over the proper line between congressional and executive authority to make war. They led to a political donnybrook.

In 1836, Texas had declared itself an independent

state under the presidency of Sam Houston, and thereafter sought annexation to the United States. Given the expansionistic fervor of the times, the proposition had wide popularity but was strongly opposed by the abolitionists, who charged that Texas— once annexed—could be carved into enough smaller states to give the South preponderant political strength. Presidents Andrew Jackson and Martin Van Buren procrastinated. Meanwhile, rebuffed by the United States, Texas turned to Europe in search of allies and commercial markets. An independent Texas that would be a buffer state against U.S. expansion, as well as a valuable source of cotton and a duty-free market, was an attractive idea to Great Britain and France. Texas concluded treaties with both nations.

When John Tyler succeeded William Henry Harrison as President in 1841, he eagerly took on the problem that Jackson and Van Buren had sidestepped. Strongly expansionistic, ardently proslavery, and more than willing to add Texas to the United States, the new President promptly reopened negotiations for annexation. Beyond this, Tyler and Secretary of State John C. Calhoun—a Southerner favoring slavery and expansion—played with the notion of rendering military assistance to Texas. In 1843, when Texas claimed it was being invaded by Mexico, Tyler tried to send the U.S. Army to lend assistance. But the plan was quickly aborted by violent congressional objection. As John Nelson, Tyler's acting secretary of state, explained in a letter to the American minister to Texas on March 11, 1843: "The employment of the Army or Navy against a foreign power, with which the United States is at peace, is not within the competency of the President."

Later that year, Tyler and Houston signed an annexation treaty which was placed before the U.S. Senate. One of the conditions of the treaty was that after signing, but before ratification, the United States would take steps to provide military and naval protection along the Gulf of Mexico and the southwestern border of Texas as a safeguard against Mexican aggression. The Senate, at odds with Tyler and Calhoun over their racial views and fearful of the potential political power of the South, defeated the annexation treaty on June 8, 1843. Nonetheless, Tyler carried out his pledge to send naval vessels to the Gulf Coast of Texas and troops to Texas' Mexican border. Legitimate presidential authority had no doubt been exceeded. But the abuse went largely unnoticed in the thunder of the presidential campaign of 1844.

In that election, the Whig party nominated Henry Clay; the Democrats chose James K. Polk to replace Tyler. Under Polk's guidance, the Democratic party modified the Tyler position, but without abandoning that vision of an endless horizon represented by the doctrine of Manifest Destiny. It paired the annexation of Oregon and the annexation of Texas, hoping to gain the support of both pro- and antislavery forces. The Whigs, on the other hand, tried to piece together a majority by not mentioning the controversial matter of Texas in their platform. Polk won handsomely, carrying every western and southwestern state except Ohio and sweeping a large Democratic majority into Congress. Now a lame duck President with a lame duck legislature, Tyler viewed the election as an endorsement for annexation. He thereupon submitted his proposal to Congress, but this time in the form of a resolution requiring only a simple majority of both houses. In early 1845, the resolution was adopted.

When Polk succeeded Tyler, he chose to interpret his popular mandate and the power of his party in the new Congress as permitting him to move beyond Texas and encroach upon additional Mexican territory—the areas currently comprising New Mexico, Arizona, California, and parts of northern Mexico. As might be expected, relations between the United States and Mexico rapidly deteriorated.

On the surface, the Polk administration was quarreling with the Mexican government over two limited issues. One was monetary: the Mexican government had ceased payment on several U.S. claims. The second related to boundaries: Texas wanted to establish the Rio Grande as the dividing line with Mexico, a line totally unacceptable to the Mexicans, who still claimed all of Texas. In fact, Polk's sights were aimed higher.

When peaceful negotiations failed, the President and his cabinet were far from disappointed. They believed that they might, at less cost, gain more concessions through war than through negotiations. Even before Polk sent a personal emissary to Mexico in an unsuccessful attempt to settle the dispute, he ordered General Zachary Taylor into the disputed region to protect the "historic" western boundary of Texas. When Polk's diplomatic mission failed, the President went to work on a message to Congress asking for a declaration of war. Before the message was delivered, news reached Washington that a group of Taylor's men had been ambushed by the Mexican army. This was Polk's Tonkin Gulf. In a revised congressional message, the President stated:

The grievous wrongs perpetrated by Mexico upon our citizens throughout a long period of years remain unredressed. . . . The cup of forbearance had been exhausted even before the recent information from the frontier of the Del Norte [Rio Grande]. But now after reiterated menaces, Mexico has passed the boundary of the United States, has invaded our territory and shed American blood upon the American soil.

President Polk then went the whole way: "War exists, and notwithstanding all our efforts to avoid it, exists by the act of Mexico herself." Nowhere did the President mention that the attack had occurred upon disputed territory. Nowhere did he suggest that there was a certain inevitability to the attack, given the fact that American troops had been sent into an area claimed by another nation. Nowhere did he acknowledge that he might have precipitated a war without consulting Congress.

The debate in the Senate took place on May 11 and 12, 1846. Expansion was the mood of the hour. Congress unsurprisingly gave the President his declaration of war. What is surprising is that there were so many voices raised against it. Senator Thomas Clayton of Delaware, for example, stated:

I have felt that these acts of the Executive ought to be condemned—I do condemn them. I think that they will be condemned by the people of the United States. By these acts we have been precipitated into a war with a friendly nation. Congress has not been consulted, nor either branch of it. The President of the United States has the power to provoke war, perhaps the power to carry on war, without the consent of Congress, but he has not the right to do it.

In the House of Representatives, Garrett Davis of Kentucky charged that it was "our own President who began this war."

Many of those who criticized Polk felt compelled to vote the funds he requested to support American men under fire. A case in point was Senator John Jordan Crittenden of Kentucky, who opposed the war but voted for the funds to prosecute it. His reasoning—so familiar to a later generation—was as follows:

> The course that has been pursued is not that generous and forbearing policy that ought to be exercised by a powerful and great republic. . . . Suppose a British army were marched right up to our boundary while angry negotiations were going on, and cannons were pointed into one of our cities. . . . I am willing now that we should act. I am willing to do anything the exigency of the case demands for the defense of the country; and that done, I think it will be our duty, as speedily as possible, to settle our differences. We are so much mightier than they are that our condescension will be noble. . . . In the meantime we are called upon for the defense of our country. That [should] be done first; but as soon as we can, and between every blow we strike, we [should] remember it fell on the head of the neighbor—every wound we inflicted was on another republican—a man we could make our friend.

As the Mexican War progressed, the Congress became more congenial to the views of Senators Clayton and Crittenden. More and more questions began to be raised about the propriety of Polk's decisions which had led to hostilities. Some eighteen months after the war had started, the House of Representatives concluded that the President had unconstitutionally begun the war, and, in effect, censured Polk. Congressman Abraham Lincoln of Illinois wrote:

> Allow the President to invade a neighboring nation, whenever he shall deem it necessary to repel an invasion, and you allow him to do so whenever he may choose to say he deems it necessary for such purpose—and you allow him to make war at pleasure. Study to see if you can fix any limit to his power in this respect, after you have given him so much as you propose.

Congress did not end the Mexican War. It did, however, raise a warning flag for those Presidents who followed Polk, that the legislature was not willing to see its constitutional warmaking powers ignored or erased.

Throughout the nineteenth century, with remarkably few exceptions, American Presidents and Congresses sought to maintain the traditional constitutional balance between the power of the executive as commander in chief and the right of the Congress, as the representative of the people, to make the great decisions committing the human and financial resources of the country to battles large or small. The United States was growing enormously in population, territory, economic might, world influence. Most of its leaders nonetheless accepted Justice Story's dictum: "The history of republics has but too fatally proved, that they are too ambitious of military fame and conquest, and too easily devoted to the views of demagogues, who flatter their pride, and betray their interests."

4

Presidential Initiatives, 1900-1918

The United States entered the twentieth century confident of the virtue of its institutions and of its impregnability. The internal disruption of the Civil War was behind it. The nation filled the continent, and its vital interests seemed to reach across the Atlantic and Pacific oceans. "Today," said President Grover Cleveland's Secretary of State, Richard Olney, "the United States is practically sovereign on this continent and its fiat is law upon the subjects to which it confines its interposition." The secretary attributed this power to "infinite resources combined with . . . isolated position" which made the United States "practically invulnerable against any or all other powers."

But what was the proper relationship between this "practically invulnerable" nation and others? It was commonly accepted that the United States had an undefined but high-minded duty to "less fortunate" countries but how was that responsibility to be expressed? To some it meant that the United States would serve itself and others best by setting an ex-

ample of the superiority of representative government, thereby inspiring others to seek similar blessings. But this seemed too passive a role to others:
the United States should *lead*, should instruct peoples not yet equipped for self-government and guide
them toward the golden way of democratic rule.

Many influences pushed the nation to choose the
latter course. First, the United States from its inception had been expansionistic. Passivity was not in its
bones; it was up and doing. American industrial and
commercial interests were acquiring vast power at
home by the turn of the century, and their predilec-
tion was for energetic, unlimited enterprise. Then,
too, the historical link between the United States and
Great Britain predisposed Americans to assume that
empire was a measure of national greatness and a test
of national worldliness and responsibility. Finally,
the writings of Charles Darwin and the later Social
Darwinists lent legitimacy to the imperialist impulse.
For the teachings of Darwin strengthened two pre-
sumptions of American foreign policy. One was that
the Anglo-Saxon was the fittest and the most likely
to prosper: who could doubt that it was more in the
national interest to be strong and assertive than weak
and dominated? The second presumption of Social
Darwinism was that the evolutionary superiority of
the English-speaking peoples made them, in a special sense, their brothers' keeper. Science and the
commandments on brotherhood were allied, and as
divinely guided guardians of humanity, Anglo-Saxons
could not be indifferent to the rest of mankind.

This convergence of interests and idealism on behalf of American imperialism was nicely summed up
by President William McKinley, when he explained

to a group of clergymen why he had decided to take the Philippine Islands from Spain:

> I walked the floor of the White House night after night until midnight; and I am not ashamed to tell you, gentlemen, that I went down on my knees and prayed Almighty God for light and guidance more than one night. And one night late it came to me this way—I don't know how it came: (1) that we could not give them back to Spain—that would be cowardly and dishonorable; (2) that we could not turn them over to France or Germany—our commercial rivals in the Orient—that would be bad business and discreditable; (3) that we could not leave them to themselves—they were unfit for self-government—and they would soon have anarchy and misrule over there worse than Spain's was; and (4) that there was nothing left for us to do but to take them all, and to educate the Filipinos, and uplift and civilize and Christianize them, and by God's grace do the very best we could by them, as our fellow-men for whom Christ also died. And then I went to bed, and went to sleep and slept soundly.

Thus joined, commerce and an ennobling unselfishness were to inspire the dispatch of forces abroad with increasing frequency. In 1900, President McKinley, on his own, sent five thousand American troops into China as part of a multinational force to put down an uprising in Peking. It was hoped that this show of force would assure an "open door" to American commerce in China, a policy that was, of course, thought to be beneficial to the Chinese, protecting them from exploitation by more rapacious foreign powers. The McKinley administration in addition justified military intervention as necessary to protect American nationals trapped in the Peking legation.

McKinley's deployment of troops during the Boxer Rebellion did have historical precedent. As previously noted, American forces had landed on foreign shores during the nineteenth century to safeguard American citizens and their property. But these earlier expeditions were for very brief periods and were usually limited to rescuing those endangered. McKinley went further. Troops henceforth would enter foreign nations not only to protect American lives, but American business and political interests as well.

It is worth noting, however, that at the turn of the twentieth-century Presidents were not indiscriminate interventionists; military power was deployed solely against the weaker nations. Just as American Presidents had always taken for granted their right to fight Indians without congressional authorization, so they "slept soundly" after initiating certain measures of "protective retaliation" against Asians, Latin Americans, and the inhabitants of various Pacific islands. Americans by and large had come to believe that force applied against less developed nations was different in kind than a war against a great power. It is highly doubtful that American naval officers would have landed in any European port—no matter how weak the nation—to protect American lives or interests without very sober debate by the entire government, including the Congress. It is unlikely that the United States would have been casual about intervening to "maintain order" in the most chaotic European nation.

In the only instance during this period where the United States actually clashed with a European nation—the Spanish-American War—the President asked Congress for a declaration of war. The seriousness of the conflict did not set it apart from others, nor the length of hostilities; the difference was in the fact that the foe was European, and so was treated under a separate set of rules. It is fair to say that President McKinley did not rush into the Spanish-American War on his own, but was shoved into it by public opinion which had been aroused by the biased reporting of the powerful Hearst and Pulitzer newspapers. For months, these two newspaper chains had fanned a jingoistic flame by printing lurid stories of Spanish concentration camps and of terrorism in Cuba.

When the American naval vessel, the *Maine,* sank after it exploded in the harbor at Havana on February 15, 1898, the war pressures became overwhelming. And yet the President was not willing to take responsibility for sending in American troops and on April 11 went to the Congress for a declaration of war:

> In the name of humanity, in the name of civilization, in behalf of endangered American interests which give us the right and the duty to speak and to act, the war in Cuba must stop. In view of these . . . considerations, I ask Congress to authorize and empower the President to take measures to secure a full and final termination of hostilities between the government of Spain and the people of Cuba, and to secure in the island the establishment of a stable government . . . and to use the military and naval forces of the United States as may be necessary for these purposes.

The American people—at least those who stayed home—reveled in the Spanish-American War. Victory after victory was reported by the Hearst and Pulitzer newspapers. The conflict was replete with cavalry charges and heroic acts. Nothing about it engendered any moral self-doubts. All Americans could congratulate themselves on their prowess in this quite picturesque war.

As for American intervention in the affairs of non-European nations, the most conspicuous instance may be seen in the relationship between the United States and much of Latin America at the turn of the century. A stern parent confronted willful and disobedient children, and once the parental role had been accepted disciplinary measures followed. In 1901, the United States sent troops into Panama, where they remained for two months to protect portage and transportation across the vital isthmus. American troops were in and out of that country several times between April and November 1902, maintaining order and protecting commercial intercourse. In 1903, President Theodore Roosevelt ordered marines into Panama during a revolt against the established government—a revolt Roosevelt had tacitly sponsored in order to change the country's leaders. The intervention was necessary, the President asserted, to maintain "free and uninterrupted transit." Roosevelt was disturbed by no diplomatic or constitutional proprieties. He stated retrospectively:

I am interested in the Panama Canal because I started it. If I had followed conventional, conservative methods, I should have submitted a dignified state paper of approximately two hundred pages to the Congress and the debate would have been going on yet, but I took the canal zone and let Congress debate, and while the debate goes on the canal does also.

Theodore Roosevelt plainly regarded his responsibility as commander in chief as a complement to his role as chief diplomatic officer of the nation. He moved American troops as it suited the aims of his foreign policy, on the assumption that the countries to which they went could not effectively fight back. In 1903, the President put U.S. forces into Honduras and the Dominican Republic. In 1906, he sent American forces into Cuba where they occupied a number of towns and villages. A provisional governor for Cuba was appointed by the United States—justified by the President in terms of a 1903 Treaty of Relations with Cuba, which was said to give the United States the right to intervene in Cuban affairs to preserve order. Although peace soon returned to Cuba, Roosevelt's temporary occupation did not end until 1909.

Roosevelt's successor, William Howard Taft, was a retiring man except when his talents as a lawyer were challenged. He was a strict constructionist of the Constitution, or so he believed. But dealing with Latin America, he was a Rooseveltian pragmatist. In an annual message to Congress in 1911, the President quoted himself and one of his letters to his chief of staff, in which he had written about the assembling of American troops on the Mexican frontier: "The assumption by the press that I contemplate intervention on Mexican soil to protect American lives or property is of course gratuitous, because I seriously doubt whether I have such authority under any circumstances." Nevertheless, in 1912 Taft sent 8 war vessels, 125 officers, and 2,600 men into Nicaragua to protect these same American interests. Cities were bombarded. The landing forces assaulted and captured several well-fortified Nicaraguan towns, thereby preserving a local government that was heavily pledged to American financial interests.

Woodrow Wilson came to office in the wake of a campaign attacking the expansionism of Roosevelt and Taft—his two opponents in the 1912 election. The appointment of William Jennings Bryan as Wilson's secretary of state seemed appropriate, for Bryan was an outspoken isolationist who called for a halt to intervention in the affairs of our neighbors. The moralistic Bryan was not, however, altogether disinterested. He wanted the United States government to help Latin America free itself from foreign, that is, European, domination.

But neither Bryan nor the President he served were destined to follow the policies with which they were earlier associated. Wilson in the end traveled the road that Roosevelt and Taft had traveled in Latin America, hoping to influence the character of sundry Latin American regimes. In the Dominican Republic, Wilson tried to prop up an unpopular President, going so far as to order our naval forces to fire upon Dominican revolutionaries who were shelling the city of Puerto Plata. American troops were dispatched to prevent fighting in Santo Domingo itself. Eventually, disorder in the Dominican Republic defied the power of local authorities to contain it, even with sporadic assistance of American firepower. The result was that in May 1916, U.S. armed forces moved into the country, and full military occupation of Santo Domingo was proclaimed on November 29, 1916. The U.S. Navy was assigned the task of managing the internal affairs of the country and did until

1924, when a treaty was concluded between the
United States and its small Caribbean neighbor.

Wilson's dealings with Haiti paralleled those with
the Dominican Republic. In the early part of his administration, the President had ordered a treaty
drafted which he hoped the government of Haiti
would sign in the interest of American investments
in that country. The treaty proposed a customs re-
ceivership under U.S. control and was designed to
counter a similar Franco-German proposal for a joint
customs arrangement in Haiti. The Wilson draft was
rejected by Haiti. In February 1915, when General
Vilbrun Guillaume Sam successfully overthrew the
Haitian government, Wilson resubmitted the treaty.
Haiti still would not agree to its terms, and within
five months the Sam regime was overthrown and Sam
himself assassinated. Wilson then ordered the U.S.S.
Washington to Port-au-Prince, ostensibly to protect
American citizens. The marines landed. In the ensu-
ing clash a number of Haitians were killed.

American forces did not depart when order was restored. The President instructed Admiral Caperton to
stay in Haiti until the long-sought treaty was signed.
The admiral imposed martial law, took over all the
functions of the government, put the President of
Haiti and its legislature on small allowances, and
seized control of the local police. Haiti ratified Wilson's treaty on September 16, 1915. The treaty was
enforced by Wilson alone for five months before the
U.S. Senate, accepting a *fait accompli*, ratified it.

Nowhere, however, was the discrepancy between
Wilsonian rhetoric and performance more marked
than in his Mexican policies. In theory, Wilson supported Mexican self-determination, and on January 8,

1915, had spoken glowingly of Mexico in a speech at
Indianapolis:

> There is one thing I have got a great enthusiasm
> about, I might almost say a reckless enthusiasm, and
> that is human liberty. . . . I want to say a word about
> Mexico, or not so much about Mexico as about our atti-
> tude towards Mexico. I hold it as a fundamental prin-
> ciple, and so do you, that every people has the right to
> determine its own form of government; and until this
> recent revolution in Mexico, until the end of the Diaz
> reign, eighty percent of the people of Mexico never
> had a 'look in' in determining who should be their
> governors or what their government should be. Now I
> am for the eighty percent! It is none of my business,
> and it is none of yours, how they go about the busi-
> ness. The country is theirs. The Government is theirs.
> And so far as my influence goes while I am President
> nobody shall interfere with them. That is what I mean
> by the great emotion, the great emotion of sympathy.

In practice, Wilson could not keep hands off Mexico's internal affairs. He opposed the Huerta regime
which had come to power in early 1913 through a
bloody coup. "I will not recognize a government of
butchers," Wilson said privately. Publicly, he refused
to send an ambassador to Mexico City. The decision
to withhold recognition because the Huerta government did not meet the President's standard introduced a new principle, or perhaps expedient, to
American foreign policy: countries would be granted
or denied diplomatic status by us according to the
kind of government they had. Huerta, along with
many of his countrymen, was appalled. Wilson in
turn was appalled when, on October 10, 1913, Huerta
arrested and imprisoned most of the upper house of

the Mexican legislature and inaugurated a full-fledged military dictatorship. Secure in his moral indignation, Wilson set out to undermine the Huerta government. He pledged American support to a revolutionary group headed by Venustiano Carranza. Wilson appears to have thought that by collaborating with Carranza, he could influence the direction of the Mexican Revolution and have a hand in shaping a new government.

On February 3, 1914, Wilson revoked the arms embargo which he had established for Mexico, thus permitting munitions to reach the Carranza forces. He then stationed U.S. naval units off Vera Cruz to block any European efforts to reinforce the Huerta government. But the Huerta government did not collapse. If anything, its resilience was strengthened. Wilson now faced the real possibility that he would have to make good on his commitment to the revolutionary forces of General Carranza. Only a pretext for intervention was needed. On April 9, 1914, several crewmen from the U.S.S. *Dolphin*, which was anchored off Tampico, Mexico, strayed into a restricted area of that city, were arrested by local Mexican authorities and paraded through the streets. As soon as the Mexican military commander for Tampico learned of the incident, the sailors were released, and the Huerta government apologized to the United States. Nonetheless, Admiral Henry Mayo, the commanding naval officer, demanded a twenty-one-gun salute of the American flag. Huerta refused—not without awareness of the irony involved in a U.S. demand to discharge an obligation of recognition although it did not recognize his government. Notes were exchanged. Within days Wilson converted a minor incident into a deliberate affront to the honor of the

United States, and on April 20, 1914, the President appeared before Congress assembled in joint session and asked for authority to use the armed forces to redress U.S. grievances against Mexico.

While Congress was deliberating this request, Wilson learned that a German steamer, the *Ypiranga,* was sailing toward Vera Cruz to unload a huge supply of munitions for Huerta. He thereupon decided to direct his naval reprisal against Vera Cruz instead of Tampico. American occupation of Vera Cruz on April 21 resulted in four hundred Mexican and one hundred American casualties. On April 22, Congress passed a joint resolution declaring that the President was "justified in the employment of armed forces of the United States to enforce his demand for unequivocal amends for certain affronts and indignities committed against the United States."

Young Felix Frankfurter was at the time working in the War Department in Washington, and years later he recalled a conversation he had then had with Judge Advocate General Enoch H. Crowder:

> "Frankfurter, I want you to help me. I've just been over to the White House—this was just after we had seized the customs house at Vera Cruz—and I'm asked to write a memorandum whether that seizure should be treated as an act of war and what its status is in international law. Will you work with me on that?"
>
> I said, "General, I'm going to ask to be excused. I don't have to work on that. I know the answer to that."
>
> "You do?"
>
> "Yes, I do."
>
> "What is the answer?"
>
> "It would be an act of war against a great nation; it isn't against a small nation."

"I can't give him that."
"I know you can't, but that's the answer." *

Public opinion was not entirely on Wilson's side. Many Americans did not think the President was justified in the reprisals against Vera Cruz. Only a few in the Wilson administration understood the action in terms of Wilson's desire to hasten the downfall of the Huerta government. Most of the press and the public viewed the occupation as an outrageous overreaction and a contradiction of the President's stated position for peace and self-determination. A flood of letters and petitions from private citizens, peace groups, Socialist organizations, labor unions, and church groups poured into the White House.

Finally, on July 15, 1914, the Huerta government fell and Carranza's forces entered Mexico City. Almost immediately, the revolutionary forces split, a faction led by Pancho Villa opposing Carranza. Wilson chose to support Villa on grounds that he would probably win and that he would be more amenable to U.S. influence. He bet on the wrong man. The Carranza forces routed Villa and pushed him northward into his native stronghold of Chihuahua.

By now, Washington had numerous experts on Mexico who offered conflicting advice. No one in the administration wanted a major war with Mexico, especially since tensions were rising in Europe and fighting might break out momentarily. Nevertheless, strong voices favored intervention. The Hearst newspapers were again thumping the jingoist drum. On

---

* *Felix Frankfurter Reminisces* (New York: Reynal and Company, 1960).

December 6, 1914, Theodore Roosevelt in the pages of the *New York Times Magazine* demanded intervention. Considerable pressure was coming from the hierarchy of the Roman Catholic church, which was violently opposed to Carranza's anticlerical views. But in the end, moderation won. Robert Lansing, the new secretary of state, convinced Wilson that the wisest course was to recognize the Carranza regime as the *de facto* government of Mexico. When Wilson did so, the Hearst papers and the Catholic press attacked him vitriolically.

But the most savage reaction to Wilson's recognition of the Carranza government came from Villa, who executed Americans in Mexico and staged murderous raids across the border into New Mexico. Coming as it did in the election year of 1916, Villa's violence set off cries in Congress for revenge. On January 15, 1916, a resolution authorizing the President to use armed forces in Mexico very nearly passed Congress, although it was opposed by the administration. It appeared that Villa was determined to draw the United States into conflict and rising anti-Villa sentiment in the United States could not be ignored. On March 9, instructions were sent to the military commander in Texas to assemble an expedition to chase Villa. A protocol between the United States and Mexico was drawn empowering either nation to pursue bandits across the international boundary. The United States initialed the protocol, declared it in force, and an expedition under the command of General John J. Pershing crossed the border on March 15, 1916.

The Carranza government was not pleased, for the protocol had not yet been ratified by one house of the Mexican legislature. But by the time it was ratified,

Pershing was deep into Mexican territory. Moreover, the U.S. expedition was far larger than anything Carranza had envisioned when he had agreed to retaliatory raids across the common border. The United States had sent a small army, not a patrol. Worse yet, Villa proved difficult to trap. The revolutionary-turned-bandit fled ever southward, pulling Pershing after him. By April 8, Pershing's forces, now 6,675 men, were three hundred miles into Mexico. The raiders had become invaders.

Almost one month after Pershing crossed the border, the Mexican government demanded that he take his troops out of the country. Caught in election-year politics, Wilson thought he could not accede to Carranza's request. As a result, complicated and protracted negotiations ensued—which were further enlivened by Villa's continued outrages against American citizens. Not until he had been reelected President and was confronting the prospect of a major war in Europe did Wilson withdraw the Pershing expedition.

The pattern of unilateral intervention by the United States in Latin America was repeated throughout the twenties. Troops were landed for brief "protection" stints in Honduras, Panama, and Guatemala. A more prolonged and controversial expedition was ordered into Nicaragua in 1926 by President Calvin Coolidge. The intervention followed local disturbances, which led Nicaragua's government to request the presence of U.S. troops. About five thousand soldiers were put ashore to set up so-called neutral zones throughout the country. These peace-keeping ventures of Coolidge—undertaken without congressional authorization—were denounced by his political opponents in Congress who railed against the President's private war and his flagrant imperialism. These attacks were not framed in terms of executive violation of the Constitution. Coolidge's opponents treated the intervention as merely unwise, or unsound. By the late 1920s, Congress had become so accustomed to thinking of the Caribbean as an American lake that it had ceased to pass judgment on presidential actions in the area.

But again, when the executive treated with the established states of Western Europe, it was another matter. So it was with World War I. Wilson at one point was "too proud to fight." He delayed his decision to enter as long as possible. But when the mounting submarine war of the North Atlantic pushed the country to the edge of decision, Wilson turned to Congress for a formal declaration of war. Wilson had no doubt that if American forces were to be used against major powers in Europe, he must have congressional sanction.

Wilson later did send American troops into Russia in the so-called Archangel expedition of 1918, without specific legislative authorization. The situation with regard to Russia was confused. During the war, shipping routes from England to north Russia had been protected to keep open Russia's two warmwater ports through which war materiel could reach the eastern front. The task of guarding ships moving to and from the Russian ports of Murmansk and Archangel had fallen largely upon the British—increasingly so as the Russian government began to disintegrate. At the time of the Bolshevik Revolution in 1917, Great Britain had a full naval squadron stationed at Murmansk.

In the months immediately preceding the revolution, a large store of armaments badly needed on the western front had been unloaded at these two Russian ports. The armaments had not been paid for by the Russians and were financed largely by U.S. and British bank credits. The Bolsheviks toward the end of 1917 renounced all credit obligations of the previous Russian government and stated that they did not propose to make reimbursements. When in February 1918 the Bolshevik government moved into Archangel, its first act was to move these military stores—for which they had no external use, since Russia had just signed a peace treaty with Germany—into the interior of the country. The British tried to regain the supplies by trading them for food, which was desperately needed by the Russians, but the offer went unheeded.

The British squadron at Murmansk had had a close working relationship with the local government—which infuriated high-ranking Russian officials—and the British general staff quickly worked out plans to establish a foothold in Russia from which military operations could be launched. There were several British motives. One was to ensure the protection of Allied arms stores. Another was to prevent a German take-over of the two ports, which the British thought likely despite the Russo-German peace agreement. Finally, the British had an interest in overthrowing the new Bolshevik government, or rather in encouraging opposition to it. An Archangel expedition was therefore viewed as a first thrust into the interior, in the direction of the Ural Mountains, that would link up with allied Czechoslovakian military forces then located in the interior of Russia, and with a Japanese army which was to move into Siberia.

Arrangements were made for half the Czech forces to move north to meet the British near Murmansk. In fact, the Czech troops never followed their instructions. Nevertheless, British planning proceeded on the assumption that the Czech forces could be counted on. American support for this allied landing was sought and the U.S. command in Europe determined that approval from Washington would be needed before such support could be given.

The request to Washington stated that American forces were necessary for the occupation of the Russian ports of Archangel and Murmansk, so as to prevent German seizure of war supplies. No mention was made of the plans for a later expedition into the interior of Russia. It was known that Wilson opposed any Siberian expedition. The President, who knew little or nothing about the military or political situation in north Russia, pondered the secret Allied request. Both Wilson and his chief military advisers were dubious that any good could come of the venture. Their dilemma was that they had turned down other previous Allied requests for intervention in Russia. Wilson felt obliged to support Great Britain, and the request regarding Murmansk seemed innocent enough. After some procrastination, Wilson finally agreed to send American troops for the limited purpose of protecting Allied war materiel. The troops were to be outfitted by the British and placed under British command.

Meanwhile, the British had gone ahead and attacked Archangel. They had done it with ease but had then been surrounded by Russian armed forces. As a result, the American troops were not sent by their British commanders to Murmansk to guard stores, but to the front at Archangel. Suddenly, to their complete bewilderment, they found themselves fighting the Russian army. Americans were participating—under British auspices and orders—in a Russian civil war. Of the five thousand-odd Americans sent to Archangel, five hundred were casualties.

Word of the extent of the Russian operation eventually reached Washington, but by then Germany was collapsing and peace was near. Little attention was given the somewhat peripheral struggle going on in northern Russia. In any case, it would be difficult to claim that Wilson was making war in Russia without congressional authority. He was opposed to intervention in Russian affairs and had not known that he was authorizing exactly that when he sent troops to Murmansk. In Wilson's eyes, he was acting as a wartime commander in chief, maneuvering against Germany, an enemy designated as such by Congress.

In retrospect, the first three decades of the twentieth century marked an enlargement of the President's power to deploy American troops abroad. And yet, this power was exercised largely in the Caribbean—and to a lesser extent, the Pacific—against small, primitive, and non-European nations. Before Franklin D. Roosevelt, it was not accepted in practice or theory that the President could initiate hostilities or respond to them at will. The guidelines of the Founding Fathers had been stretched but not scrapped.

5

Presidential Omniscience

When Franklin D. Roosevelt was elected President in 1932, there were 16 million workers unemployed, the average weekly wage had fallen to less than eighteen dollars, and the people hungered for forceful leadership. They got it. To a majority of Americans, Roosevelt was a savior, and the judgment of a savior is to be trusted. It is little wonder then that in the anxious days of 1940 and 1941, FDR was able to expand constitutional constraints more than any man before him in the White House. His administrations were a turning point in the history of presidential-congressional conflicts over the war powers provisions of the Constitution.

It did not seem so at the start. The Good Neighbor policy of the President and Secretary of State Cordell Hull was an explicit renunciation of the right of one nation to intervene in the affairs of another. In his first inaugural address, FDR said that the United

States stood "ready to carry on in the spirit of that application of the Golden Rule by which we mean the true goodwill of the true good neighbor." This high-mindedness was made explicit by the decision to abandon intervening in Cuba in order to preserve the independence and domestic tranquility of that country. Shortly thereafter, American marines were removed from Nicaragua and Haiti. In 1938, when Mexico nationalized foreign oil holdings, Roosevelt demanded compensation but did not contemplate military action. In 1940, the President permitted the Dominican Republic to begin collecting its own tariffs, which for thirty-five years had been collected by the United States.

There was nothing in the Good Neighbor policy which represented any presidential judgment about the right to use American troops without congressional authorization. From Roosevelt's standpoint, the policy was a diplomatic strategy to improve relations with our southern neighbors.

In their totality the Roosevelt administrations swung the balance heavily to the side of the chief executive. Under the President's skillful guidance, the United States edged toward World War II without congressional authorization and indeed without congressional support. No one can plausibly claim that if FDR had not done what he did in 1940 and 1941 the United States would have stayed out of the war. Undoubtedly, we would have intervened to put an end to Nazi tyranny. At any rate, the question was settled for us by the Japanese attack on Pearl Harbor. And yet it must be recalled that the President committed the nation to conflict before he sought, or could have received, congressional authorization. Whether his tactics were in violation of the Constitution can be disputed; certainly they were in violation of specific congressional statute. In the fall of 1940 for example, in order to help the Allies, Roosevelt agreed to deliver a flotilla of renovated destroyers to Great Britain in exchange for military bases on British soil. Attorney General Robert Jackson defended the President's move as legal under his power as commander in chief to "dispose" the armed forces. In fact, the President had disposed of part of the armed forces to a foreign nation—which probably was not legally permissible.

Similarly, in April 1941, after Germany invaded Denmark, President Roosevelt occupied Greenland in apparent contradiction of the intent of Congress. Two congressionally enacted statutes, the Reserves Act of 1940 and the Selective Service Act of 1940, barred the use of U.S. Reserves and draftees outside the "Western Hemisphere." While President Roosevelt did not technically violate the congressional restriction, he was moving the country toward belligerency against the express will of Congress.

In July 1941, U.S. troops occupied Iceland. The President informed the Congress of that fact on the same day. In November 1941, Roosevelt ordered American troops to occupy Dutch Guiana—by agreement with the Dutch government-in-exile. The President neither asked for nor received congressional consent. By the middle of 1941 U.S. ships on presidential order were secretly convoying allied supply ships across the Atlantic despite FDR's public stand against convoying, and despite an express congressional prohibition against such use of the American navy. In describing the various steps taken by Roosevelt during 1940 and 1941, Professor Ruhl J. Bartlett commented:

> It seems beyond doubt that the President had placed the United States in a state of war without congressional authority. . . . [H]e not only impinged on the right of Congress to declare war but also violated existing law.

Of course Roosevelt saw danger ahead. He had strong opinions as to what had to be done to defend the national interest. Certainly, his perception of the threat was more accurate and enlightened than that of an isolationist Congress. Yet, on balance, are we to salute FDR for the means he used to lead the country to war? Do we wish to say, as Merlo Pusey has posed the current dilemma, "that Congress has the exclusive power to declare war, except when the President concludes that it is unwilling to do so, and in that event the power shall pass to the President?" (*The Way We Go to War*). I cannot respond affirmatively to that question. For the consequence of Roosevelt's taking upon himself powers that he did not possess, or powers he chose not to share with Congress, was an affirmation of presidential omnipotence for which a high price has been paid. In succeeding years Congress and the public became more and more vulnerable to presidential claims that only the executive branch knew enough to be able to make accurate judgments about foreign policy. Congress was told it must not interfere, because its collective judgment was untrustworthy on so complex and momentous a matter as war. And if Congress did interfere, the chief executive could always find extralegal ways to get around the will of the legislators. The dilemma thus posed for responsible legislators has been awesome. It is not a dilemma that the Founding Fathers intended that Congress should face.

Since World War II, Congress has never been of one mind about its constitutional war powers. On the one hand, the legislature has made attempts to lay down broad principles—in the context of treaty provisions and resolutions—to restate and reassert its right to determine when and against whom U.S. troops could be committed. On the other hand, when Congress has been confronted with specific situations, it has more often than not defended overreaching chief executives, out of misguided definitions of loyalty to party or country. Nowhere was this dichotomy better illustrated than in Harry S Truman's remarkable two terms.

Four months after he assumed office, Truman, with one monumental decision, ended a world war and opened a new era. A White House statement issued on August 6, 1945, described the incredible new weapon that had been unleashed the previous day on the people of Hiroshima, Japan: "It is an atomic bomb. It is a harnessing of the basic power of the universe. The force from which the suns draws its power has been loosed against those who brought war to the Far East." From then on the decision to go to war would take on a new, more awesome meaning. The ultimate risk was no longer only the destruction of a functioning society, it was now the destruction of the world itself.

Truman accepted responsibility for the most consequential military decision in history. Whatever controversy surrounds his choice, and it is debated to this day, there can be no doubt that he acted legally.

He was performing his constitutional role as commander in chief in a declared war. But, despite its clear legal correctness, Truman's decision probably did have an impact on the war clause of the Constitution.

The atomic bomb changed the attitude of Americans toward the warmaking process. No other single factor was more responsible for the modern-day myth of the superiority of presidential decision-making. From that time on, Presidents were perceived as larger than life, and the executive branch was seen as the repository of all knowledge, especially in foreign affairs. The tough and lonely choices made by the one man who occupied the White House became a part of the American legend.

But Congress had not yet succumbed completely to myth during the first Truman administration. In fact, even before the end of World War II, Congress was actively asserting its war powers.

Thus, when the Congress enacted the United Nations Participation Act in 1945, it carefully restricted the President's authority to negotiate agreements with the United Nations, under which American troops might be assigned to peace-keeping tasks around the world. Although the President might sign such agreements, they were to be "subject to the approval of Congress by appropriate Act or joint resolution." The Participation Act specifically stated that "nothing herein contained shall be construed as an authorization to the President by the Congress to make available to the Security Council . . . armed forces, facilities, and assistance provided for in such special agreement or agreements." Once Congress approved a particular participation agreement, no further legislative action would be necessary to commit troops to a peace-keeping force. Congress believed, no doubt correctly, that to require its approval of specific missions would undermine the entire peace-keeping system as it was envisioned in the United Nations Charter.

The Truman administration presumably found this formula satisfactory. In a message read on the Senate floor July 28, 1945, the President stated: "When any such agreement or agreements are negotiated, it will be my purpose to ask the Congress by appropriate legislation to approve them." *

Although approximately three years separated the agreements, the North Atlantic Treaty was similar to the United Nations Participation Act in that it too provided for congressional participation in all subsequent decisions to deploy or commit American troops. Negotiated between the United States and most of the nations of Western Europe in 1949, the treaty stated that the signatories would regard an attack upon one of them as an attack upon all. The question arose, naturally, as to whether this provision meant that an aggressive attack on a European signatory would automatically plunge the United States into war, or whether the consent of Congress was required.

The legislative history of the document indicates that the Senate believed the latter to be the case. Several senators worked with the State Department in negotiating the treaty. One of those active in the drafting was Senator Walter F. George of Georgia, who later related that it was he who insisted upon the addition of Article 11, which read in part: "The

* There have been no negotiations such as those referred to in the Participation Act, and no troop commitment accords between particular countries and the United Nations have ever been signed.

treaty shall be ratified and its provisions carried out by the parties in accordance with their respective constitutional processes." Senator George, the ranking member of the Foreign Relations Committee, told his colleagues:

> The Secretary of State, who was the spokesman for the administration, then interpreted the words "constitutional processes" to mean congressional approval insofar as a declaration of war or the employment of our troops in any foreign country was concerned, and that language was designedly inserted into the treaty.

Senator George's interpretation was supported by Senator Tom Connally of Texas, also a member of the Foreign Relations Committee. In a lengthy exchange on the Senate floor, Connally replied to a question from Senator Arthur Watkins of Utah:

> MR. WATKINS. I want to know if Article 11 means that the provisions of this treaty are to be implemented by the Congress.
> MR. CONNALLY. How does the Senator think they are to be implemented? Does he think they are to be implemented by the bootblack in the barber shop? Of course, they are to be implemented by the Congress, within its constitutional powers.

However, once the NATO treaty and the Participation agreement were approved by the Congress, the carefully drafted expression of Congress' constitutional powers was ignored by President Truman, and Congress did not insist on their enforcement. Truman sent U.S. "advisory" troops to Greece and Turkey on his own initiative—whatever the wording of the NATO treaty. When the Korean crisis came to

the United Nations the President again bypassed the
Congress. In deploying troops to Korea in 1950, Truman acted without an authorization of any kind.
American air and naval support were ordered into
the southern half of that divided country to meet
Communist aggression from the north, before any
formal presentation by the President to the Congress of the facts of the Korean situation. The President could hardly claim he was responding to an
attack upon the United States or any of its citizens.
Neither could he claim to have even acted under a
mutual defense treaty, since there was none.

The President justified his intervention by reference to our obligation to the United Nations. But at
the time Truman initially committed American forces
to South Korea, he lacked any United Nations support or mandate. Only after Truman acted did the Security Council—in the absence of the Soviet Union,
which was temporarily not attending council sessions—pass a U.S.-sponsored resolution calling for
volunteer national units to repel the invaders. More
importantly, even if this resolution had preceded the
President's deployment of troops, it would not have
justified his action. For the United States had never
formally committed any troops to the United Nations;
there were no forces available which could be dispatched without congressional assent.

On June 27, 1950, Mr. Truman stated:

> The Security Council of the United Nations called
> upon the invading troops to cease hostilities and to
> withdraw to the 38th parallel. This they have not
> done, but on the contrary have pressed the attack. The
> Security Council called upon all members of the

United Nations in the execution of this resolution. In these circumstances I have ordered United States air and sea forces to give the Korean government troops cover and support.

That statement implied that Mr. Truman's move followed the United Nations resolution. It did not. The statement also implied that the President had the power, without any further congressional authorization, to send troops once the United Nations had acted. The President did not. Senator Robert Taft of Ohio noted that the President had "simply usurped authority, in violation of the laws and the Constitution when he sent troops to Korea." Senator Arthur Watkins argued that "the United States is at war by order of the President." The administration's response was a characteristically bold defense. In an unsigned article in the Department of State *Bulletin*, the position was taken that "the President, as Commander in Chief of the Armed Forces of the United States, has full control over the use thereof." There followed an assertion that Truman had exercised the "traditional power of the President to use the armed forces of the United States without consulting Congress." No precedents were cited, perhaps because the assertions had no constitutional and little historical validity.

The Truman administration asserted that if it had not immediately sent troops into South Korea, that nation would have fallen to the army of North Korea. President Truman, as a practical matter, was probably correct in that assertion. But it should be noted that at the time of the attack, Congress sympathized with South Korea's plight and would in all probability have endorsed supportive action. Moreover, if the United States was able to take its case to the Security Council the day following the invasion, it could certainly have taken its case to Congress.

Dwight D. Eisenhower took a rather different tack. A military hero, Eisenhower was as devoted to the principle of civilian control over the military as any President in our history. He believed that a President should assure himself of congressional support for whatever course he might be forced to take. Early in his term, President Eisenhower was beseeched by France to supply military aid, including manpower, to the French army, then enmeshed in its torturous struggle in Indochina. When the President was asked at a press conference if he would authorize such aid, he replied: "There is going to be no involvement of America in war unless it is a result of the constitutional process that is placed upon Congress to declare it."

Eisenhower's determination to involve the Congress accomplished several different ends. First, his administrations can be said to have met and passed the traditional test of constitutionality. Second, Eisenhower found that by explaining situations to Congress which seemed to risk U.S. military engagement, he was able to use Congress as a sounding board—informing himself about the political temper of the country and informing and rallying the American people. Third, by laying before Congress potentially dangerous situations, he notified a potential enemy that the United States took the situation seriously and might well act. On occasion, this sort of warning precluded the need for further steps.

On December 1, 1954, the United States signed a security pact with the Republic of China, based on Taiwan. The Republic of China claimed as part of its territory several offshore islands close to mainland China, most notably Quemoy and Matsu. These islands were also claimed by the People's Republic of China. The security pact between the United States and the Republic of China did not specifically include these offshore islands in its guarantee of protection to Taiwan. But almost immediately after the pact was signed, the islands came under heavy bombardment by the mainland Chinese. By January 1955, the island of Ichiang had been "liberated" by the Communists. Eisenhower looked for a way to inform the Peking government that it could not count on continuing these military assaults without serious risk of retribution. He did not, however, want to pledge the United States to a defense of the islands under any and all circumstances. The President therefore asked Congress on January 24 for a mandate allowing him to do whatever might prove needed and to "remove any doubt regarding our readiness to fight, if necessary, to preserve the vital stake of the free world in a free Formosa. . . ."

Eisenhower's message read in part:

I do not suggest that the United States enlarge its defensive obligations beyond Formosa and the Pescadores as provided by the treaty now awaiting ratification. But unhappily, the danger of armed attack directed against that area compels us to take into account closely related localities and actions which under certain conditions, might determine the failure or the success of such an attack. The authority that may be accorded by the Congress would be used only in situations which are recognizable as parts of, or def-

inite preliminaries to, an attack against the main positions of Formosa and the Pescadores.

The President did not distinguish what he could do
on his own in this situation, and what actions would
require congressional authorization. His point was
that in such a case the line was too difficult to draw
and that the most effective approach legally, diplo-
matically, and militarily was for Congress and the
President to declare their joint commitment to a possible military venture, before events made any such
venture necessary. There would then be no recrimi-
nations that could split the country and no uncertain-
ties abroad. To quote again from the President's message:

> Until Congress can act I would not hesitate, so far as
> my constitutional powers extend, to take whatever
> emergency action might be forced upon us in order to
> protect the rights and security of the United States.
> However, a suitable congressional resolution would
> clearly and publicly establish the authority of the
> President as Commander in Chief to employ the
> Armed Forces of this Nation promptly and effectively
> for the purposes indicated if in his judgment it be-
> came necessary.

A Taiwan Resolution extending the requested authority to the President was quickly passed by the
Congress. Its adoption could have marked a return to
congressional participation in decisions to go to war.
Unfortunately, it did not, largely because Congress
itself failed to follow up this promising opportunity.
The next time that the Congress was asked to consider pledging American military might, it virtually
abrogated its constitutional duty.

The near renunciation occurred in 1957, with the

endorsement by Congress of the so-called Middle
East Resolution. The British and French had already
surrendered control of the Suez Canal and withdrawn their forces from the Middle East, leaving in
their wake an unstable political situation. Eisenhower, influenced by Secretary of State John Foster
Dulles, thought he should have authority to negotiate
economic and military aid agreements with various
Middle Eastern nations. It was not that he wished to
fish in troubled water; he wanted to keep them free
from Communist pollution. He wanted a clear mandate to respond promptly to any request by any
one of these nations for military help against such
aggression.

The President came to Congress personally, on
January 5, 1957, to state his case. Some interpreted
his request for power to use American military force
as an attempt to preempt congressional authority.
Other congressmen, by now accustomed to executive
preemption, argued that the President did not need
the resolution, that he had sufficient power as commander in chief to use the armed forces anywhere to
protect the vital interests of the United States. The
"liberal" Senate position was that the United States
was best served by a strong President and that executive power should not be hamstrung. It was considered a liberal victory when the resolution was
stripped of the word "authorize," and rewritten as
merely a statement of foreign policy. In so doing,
Congress implied that the President need not ask its
permission to do what he had in mind. Thus, the resolution read in part:

. . . if the President determines the necessity thereof,
the United States is prepared to use armed forces to

assist any nation or group of nations requesting assistance against armed aggression from any country controlled by international communism: *Provided,* that such employment shall be consonant with the treaty obligations of the United States and with the Charter of the United Nations.

The Middle East Resolution was unique in the history of the controversy over the war power provisions of the Constitution. It offered the spectacle of a President coming to Capitol Hill for authority, and Congress replying: "Why ask us? Do it yourself. You have all the power you need."

Fortunately, a misreading by one Congress of the language of the Constitution does not give the President power he does not possess. Nevertheless, one would hesitate to condemn a chief executive—after the Middle East Resolution of 1957—for thinking that Congress was more than willing to tolerate a decisive commander in chief. And when John F. Kennedy succeeded to the presidency in 1961, he was ready to take Congress at its word and to consolidate power in the White House at the expense of the legislature. Kennedy believed in the activist theory of presidential leadership, a belief perhaps inspired by his study of Franklin Roosevelt's presidency. If Congress wished to be sheltered from military responsibilities, Kennedy was perfectly willing to oblige.

During the days preceding the Bay of Pigs invasion of Cuba, Kennedy did not consult Congress. Approximately two hours before the invasion was to begin, he informed leaders of the House and the Senate of events which were to transpire. When the invasion failed, Kennedy courageously admitted his mistake in supporting an ill-conceived effort to overthrow the government of Fidel Castro. What he did not admit— and what few in Congress saw fit to tell him—was that he alone did not have the authority to commit the military might of the United States. As the Kennedy administration labored in 1961–62 to isolate Cuban communism and stop it from spreading throughout Latin America, Congress demanded no policy-making role. Rather, it was eager to help the President do it himself. Kennedy responded coolly, indicating that if Congress wished to pass a resolution in support of his emerging Cuban policy, it would not be unwelcome. But in the President's opinion, no resolution was required. If the legislators felt that it must act, however, then it should simply endorse the President's broad conception of his powers as commander in chief.

The actual resolution, which was introduced with administration blessings, stated that "the President of the United States is supported in his determination and possesses all necessary authority" to prevent the creation of offensive military bases in Cuba, to use the armed forces to prevent the exportation of communism from Cuba into the rest of the hemisphere, and to work for a return of self-determination in Cuba.

The phrase "possesses all necessary authority" went too far, however, and evoked a negative reaction from some of the most powerful men in the Senate. At a hearing on the resolution, Senators Richard Russell of Georgia, Henry Jackson of Washington, Stuart Symington of Missouri, Wayne Morse of Oregon, and Frank Church of Idaho, expressed alarm. Any such resolution, they said, should state that all the proposed actions were "authorized" by Congress. Secretary of State Dean Rusk countered by claiming that the resolution was not intended to "change the constitutional responsibilities" of Congress and that the language in it did not do so.

This disagreement over wording was finally resolved by changing the resolution into a declaration of national policy. As amended, it said that the United States was "determined" to do all of the things that the administration's proposed resolution had suggested. Thus, it neither authorized nor sanctioned anything. It simply put on record the government's position on Cuba.

When the Cuban missile crisis broke one month later, the resolution was used by the President to justify his quarantine of the shipment of missiles to Cuba. Kennedy's proclamation, the "Interdiction of the Delivery of Offensive Weapons to Cuba," relied primarily on the resolution—although without rejecting the President's right to act under his powers as commander in chief. In a speech to the nation on October 22, Kennedy hedged a bit when he said he was issuing his proclamation under the authority entrusted to him by the Constitution, "as that authority had been endorsed by . . . resolution of the Congress." It is probably fair to say that in the President's opinion no congressional assent was needed. But if Congress offered assent, he was prepared to turn that to his advantage.

On balance, the Taiwan, Middle East, and Cuban resolutions weakened the will and the power of Congress in dealing with presidential claims of authority. By enacting these resolutions, framed in the broadest language and devoid of time limitations, the Congress handed the chief executive a multiple-use tool. The resolutions led us inexorably toward the nadir of congressional responsibility.

6

Vietnam

Explanations of historical events chase each other backward into time. There is no beginning at the beginning, for we can't be sure where the beginning is. Nevertheless, the Vietnam story for America starts somewhere immediately after World War II, when the government of the United States decided *not* to take an active part in resolving the Indochina conflict. The colonies of France in Indochina had been occupied by Japan, though there was resistance by our French allies and by the Vietnamese. A loose federation of Communists and nationalists under the leadership of Ho Chi Minh—the League for the Independence of Vietnam (the Viet Minh)—was waging an underground battle against the Japanese, a guerrilla war supported by the U.S. Office of Strategic Services (OSS).

The defeat of Germany and Japan preoccupied our policy planners, and little thought was given to the possibility that the French and the Viet Minh might, in the postwar period, be at odds over the future of Vietnam. There is some evidence that Roosevelt and

Stalin discussed at Yalta whether to establish a United Nations trusteeship over Indochina and Korea, thus precluding their return to colonial status. FDR was no friend of colonialism. But no formal policy for Indochina had been set by the time of Roosevelt's death, and President Truman could not claim to have been privy to Roosevelt's thinking on the matter.

At the Potsdam Conference in July and August 1945, Truman acquiesced to a secret interim arrangement for Indochina, permitting Chinese nationalist forces to occupy Indochina north of the Sixteenth Parallel and British occupation south of that line. It was assumed that the French would eventually resume their earlier dominance of the entire region. Within a few months after the surrender of the Japanese, French officials and French troops returned to Indochina—and found a quite different political situation than the one they had left. On the day of the Japanese surrender, Ho Chi Minh liberated Hanoi and entered that city as a popular hero. American personnel attached to the Office of Strategic Services had participated, and an American flag was flown in Hanoi by the OSS. The extent of Ho's identification with the United States can be seen in the Declaration of Independence which he issued on September 2, 1945: "All men are created equal. They are endowed by their creator with certain inalienable rights, among these are Life, Liberty and the Pursuit of Happiness." Ho was preparing to set up an indigenous government in Vietnam and appears to have believed he could count on the backing of the United States. In 1945 and 1946, he appealed repeatedly to the Truman administration for aid. The appeals went unanswered.

Forced to deal with Ho, the French proposed that the provinces of Annam and Tonkin—the present-day North Vietnam—be incorporated into a "free state" within the French Union and have its own legislature, its own army and control over its own finances. Ho's dominance over this gerrymandered state would be recognized. In contrast, the future of Cochin China—present-day South Vietnam—would be decided by a plebiscite held at some unspecified time. Meanwhile, the French would remain. This offer to Ho Chi Minh carried a price tag: Ho had to agree not to oppose the return of French troops to Indochina for a period of five years. Over the opposition of some of his colleagues, Ho accepted this condition, along with a temporary division of the Vietnamese state. Perhaps he was persuaded that France would before long abandon her colonial policy—as Great Britain was to do elsewhere in Asia—and allow all of Vietnam to fall under his provisional government. No doubt Ho was also influenced by his assessment that his army could not at that time defeat the French forces.

The new Constitution of France, proclaimed in October 1946, shattered Ho's hopes. In that document, all of Vietnam was named as an "associate state" of the French Union and as such denied any local autonomy. The new high commissioner to Vietnam, Admiral Georges Thierry d'Argenlieu, proved an old-fashioned colonialist. Ho Chi Minh believed he had been betrayed; in turn, the French colonial administration felt threatened by the increasingly hostile attitude of Ho and his growing coalition. Misunderstandings were inevitable, and before long there were violent exchanges between the two sides. Ho turned to terrorism; the French retaliated.

The Truman administration paid little attention to these disputes; its central concern was the political and economic instability of Western Europe and the rise of Russian power in Eastern Europe. No word was passed to France urging restraint, nor was any effort made to influence Ho Chi Minh. Truman wanted to strengthen French resistance to communism at home, and to build a strong front against Communist dangers in the rest of Europe. Those being its priorities, it was natural that the Truman administration would be inclined to support France in Vietnam by not opposing the status quo.

The shock waves of the war in Vietnam were felt in Paris. In 1948, France suggested that the states of Annam, Tonkin, and Cochin China could, if they wished, form a single state of Vietnam which would enjoy complete local autonomy within the French Union. Ho Chi Minh and his followers viewed this as an effort to retard their country's movement toward complete independence and rejected it.

Bao Dai, the former emperor of Annam, embraced the French idea enthusiastically.* He quickly led a band of Vietnamese nationalists into negotiations with the French, who accepted Bao Dai, as a legitimate representative of the Vietnamese people, on grounds that he was a nominal member of Ho's anticolonial coalition and the former hereditary ruler of part of the nation. Thus, Bao Dai became the chief executive of a new "phantom nation" composed of all three Vietnamese provinces. This enlarged, so-called free state, within the French Union but supposedly moving toward independence, was ridiculed by the Viet

---

* Bao Dai had abdicated power in August 1945 when Ho Chi Minh entered Hanoi, and had gone into a form of exile shuttling between France and Hong Kong in the following months.

Minh from its inception. Ho Chi Minh, the single greatest political power in the country, remained outside. The civil war did not taper off; it intensified.

By now the United States had shifted from passive acquiescence in the French position to active support of its campaign against Ho whom Washington had come to regard as one more aggressive threat to the Free World. In a sense, Ho fell victim to the anti-Communist current then running so swiftly in the United States.

By 1950, the Soviet Union had exploded its first nuclear device. Eastern Europe was a collection of police states, all of which (Yugoslavia excepted) danced to a Russian tune. Communist parties were challenging moderate governments in Italy and France. China came under the control of its Communist revolutionaries. A Communist insurrection struck Malaya. The Huk guerrillas were harassing the government of the Philippines. To most Americans, all of these events appeared interconnected; an international Communist conspiracy was on the march, intent upon world domination. And when, in 1950, North Korean forces crossed the Thirty-eighth Parallel, the United States abruptly turned to Asia—rather than Europe—as the battleground between democracy and communism. No more territory could be allowed to pass behind the iron—or bamboo—curtain.

In June 1950, Harry Truman took the first step down the long road to Vietnam. In the aftermath of the Korean invasion, he included Vietnam on his list of Asian nations where an American military presence would have to be found. Accordingly, on June 27 the President stated: "I have directed acceleration in the furnishing of military assistance to the forces of France and the Associated States in Indochina and the dispatch of a military mission to provide close working relations with these forces." * The President then sent a small contingent of American forces into the Vietnam war zone, in support of one combatant, neither consulting nor obtaining congressional authorization before doing so. Truman was operating in that no-man's-land between his power as commander in chief, and Congress' power to make war. In retrospect, he may have exceeded the limits of his constitutional authority.

After the Chinese entered the Korean struggle, the United States signed a Mutual Defense Assistance Agreement with France, whereby both nations agreed to provide military aid to all of Indochina, including Vietnam. In 1951, our military aid to that area amounted to more than 500 million dollars. And on September 7, 1951, the Truman administration further agreed to give aid directly to the Vietnamese, bypassing the government in Paris. As a side effect, the size of the American establishment in Vietnam markedly increased; many civilians in various capacities were added to the military adviser group already present.

During the transition period after the 1952 American election, warnings were passed onto prospective Eisenhower administration officials of the seriousness of the situation in Indochina. The possibility of overt Chinese intervention—such as had occurred in Korea—was stressed. The incoming secretary of state, John Foster Dulles, shared the outlook

* If June 27, 1950, marks the beginning of the American military mission in Indochina, there is no similar indication of when the American military assistance effort began, since Truman's statement was that he was "accelerating" that effort. Few Americans were aware there was any assistance effort to be accelerated.

of his predecessor, Dean Acheson: the world was divided into two major power blocs locked in seemingly eternal combat. To this view Dulles brought a heightened fervor: those who were not with us were against us—an attitude shared by Vice President Richard Nixon; the chairman of the Joint Chiefs of Staff, Admiral Arthur Radford, and the majority leader of the Senate, Republican William Knowland of California.

How, given those circumstances, could there have been any radical reassessment of the wisdom of helping the French put down an insurrection in Vietnam? President Eisenhower, having no wish to commit American troops to any Asian war, was, at the same time, unwilling to be associated with the loss of more real estate to a Communist-associated government. As the Vietnam situation deteriorated, American aid to the French and its puppet Vietnamese government soared.

Despite this very substantial level of support— $1,133,000,000 in money, advisers to train the Vietnamese national army, service crews to handle American combat planes flown by French pilots—the French army was unable to make much headway in its struggle against Ho Chi Minh's irregular forces. In 1953, Ho's troops opened a new offensive, moving north along the Chinese border and destroying one French stronghold after another until the entire Chinese border was open—permitting new support forces, supplies, and material to pour freely across it. In the face of these setbacks, Paris petitioned for more direct military assistance. Somewhat surprisingly, considering Eisenhower's personal aversion to having American soldiers fight in an Asian war, the request was not automatically turned down. Instead the administration gave very serious consideration to the possibility of direct U.S. intervention on the side of the French.

Support for such intervention came from well-placed persons in the administration, the vice president, the secretary of state, and the chairman of the Joint Chiefs of Staff. They and others were instrumental in having drafted a presidential message to the Congress seeking authorization to enter the war. Informal consultations between administration officials and the leadership of the Senate and the House disclosed, however, that the Congress was unlikely to favor intervention unless there was allied support for it, particularly support by the British. And when the British in 1954 once again proved unwilling to back up the French, Eisenhower pulled back from any direct U.S. military action. To Secretary of State Dulles, the President's decision was disappointing, though Dulles' determination to prevent a Communist take-over in Indochina was undiminished.

Continuing military setbacks in the field were meanwhile fueling discontent in France, and the resounding French defeat at Dienbienphu, after a siege of fifty-six days, broke the French will to carry on. The government in Paris was ready to make peace with the Viet Minh, and to that end the Geneva Conference was convened on April 26. Its purpose was to legitimize the Viet Minh victory in Indochina, but to do it without humiliating the colonial power. The conference's solution was to partition Vietnam at the Seventeenth Parallel, giving the northern portion to Ho and his forces and the southern portion to Bao Dai and his forces. As might have been expected, this compromise was initially resisted by both Bao Dai and Ho Chi Minh. The Western powers set out to convince Bao Dai that they were salvaging all they could from the wreckage. Ho was pressured to accept the compromise by China and the Soviet Union, who thought it prudent to conclude negotiations while Premier Mendès-France was in power in France. Ho was told that the agreement had the virtue of ending the war, while allowing him to consolidate his strength in the north. And since the Geneva accord provided that free elections would be held throughout Vietnam within two years, the Communist powers could in good faith assure Ho that his regime would win through the elective process.

The participants in the Geneva Conference, including the representatives of the two Vietnamese governments, issued two documents at the end of the conference. Provisions for a demarcation line, a demilitarized zone, and the other technicalities of French military withdrawal were put into a document called the "Cessation of Hostilities in Viet Nam" that was signed by the French and the Viet Minh. The political arrangements, including future elections, were put into a "Final Declaration of the Geneva Conference" that was signed by no one. The foreign ministers of the attending nations only expressed their support for its provisions. The United States refused to go even that far, merely stating that it recognized the existence of the documents. Thus, the accord on free elections throughout Vietnam was never accepted by Washington as binding.

In fact, Secretary Dulles made no secret of his distaste for the Geneva compromise. He, as well as the President, thought that in any general election Ho Chi Minh would win a resounding victory, and the Vietnam domino would topple. Given a rather free reign by Eisenhower, Dulles proceeded to arrange for the establishment of a Southeast Asian Treaty Organization, a defense alignment patterned roughly upon the NATO alliance in Western Europe. SEATO, however, proved little more than a legal pretext for U.S. aid to anti-Communist regimes in the Pacific. The treaty was signed by the United States, Great Britain, France, Australia, New Zealand, the Philippines, Pakistan, and Thailand just forty-nine days after the Geneva Conference ended. A separate protocol to SEATO designated Laos, Cambodia, and the "free territory under the jurisdiction of the State of Vietnam" as subject to the provisions of the treaty. The important part of the treaty was Article IV, Sections 1 and 2 which read:

> Each Party recognizes that aggression by means of armed attack in the Treaty area against any of the Parties or against any State or Territory which the Parties by unanimous agreement may hereafter designate, would endanger its own peace and safety, and agrees that it will in that event act to meet the common danger in accordance with its constitutional processes.
>
> If, in the opinion of any of the Parties, the inviolability or the integrity of the territory or the sovereignty or political independence of any Party, in the Treaty area or of any other State or Territory to which the provisions of Paragraph 1 of this Article from time to time apply is threatened in any way other than armed attack or is affected or threatened by any fact or situation which might endanger the peace of the area, the Parties shall consult immediately in order to agree on measures which should be taken for the common defense.

The SEATO treaty, like the NATO treaty before it, was not envisioned by the Congress that consented to it as being self-triggering. Any commitment of

American forces to combat under the terms of the treaty was to be contingent upon congressional approval. Such were the "constitutional processes" of the U.S. government.

But wars do not always begin with the dispatch of troops. They begin with more subtle investments of dollars and advisers. By 1955, American commitments were far-reaching. To a large extent, Washington's faith in the viability of the government of South Vietnam rested upon faith in the competence of Ngo Dinh Diem, premier of Vietnam by appointment of Bao Dai. Diem was called the George Washington of his nation. The American press pictured him as the effective democratic alternative to a Communist regime in an underdeveloped country. Throughout 1954 and 1955, there was reason to be optimistic about Diem. With some U.S. prodding, largely from the Central Intelligence Agency, a program of land reform was adopted. Economic progress began to be visible. Political stability seemed to be on the rise as Diem moved efficiently to eliminate his opposition. By contrast, Ho Chi Minh's rule in the north appeared repressive. To all appearances, his collectivization policies were unnecessarily harsh, and his efforts to put down indigenous protest were brutal.

On October 23, 1955, Ngo Dinh Diem deposed Bao Dai and there followed a referendum in which 98 percent of the voters of South Vietnam pledged their loyalty to Diem. It was not exactly a free election, but on October 26, the Republic of Vietnam was proclaimed, with Diem as its first President.

The more powerful President Diem became, the more unwilling he was to work within the guidelines of the Geneva agreements. Attempts by the north to regularize economic and postal relationships were rebuffed. On July 20, 1955, when negotiations leading to national elections were supposed to start, Diem flatly rejected the concept of any elections at all until "conditions of freedom" prevailed throughout all of Vietnam. With no opposition from the United States, Diem soon took the position that the Geneva accords had been adopted only by the North Vietnamese and the French, and that his government was in no way bound by them.

To Ho Chi Minh and the Viet Cong—the underground organization of the Viet Minh which had been left in the south in skeleton form after the Geneva agreements—the situation had become intolerable. The elections they had expected to win had been thrown aside. A weak French presence had been replaced by the United States. New economic and social policies showed promise of dissipating South Vietnamese internal discontent. The Viet Cong decided on full-scale harassment and terrorism throughout South Vietnam.

Diem's reaction was harsh, force was met by force, brutalities were matched by brutalities. Ever more rigid controls were clamped upon the population. Diem soon sacrificed land and other social reforms to military requirements. Simultaneously, he boosted requests to the United States for all possible kinds of aid.

He was not disappointed. Our policy planners were proud of Diem, proud of themselves for having averted a Communist take-over in 1954–55. Financial and military assistance were stepped up. Those who expressed concern over Diem's retreat from economic and social reform were brushed aside; after all, Diem was fighting a war.

On the judgment of the Eisenhower administration, this was a moment when Diem had to be shored up in his efforts to consolidate control over South Vietnam. The government of Ho Chi Minh for its part viewed the insurrection as the alternative to an unsuccessful policy of self-restraint. To Ho, it was clear that national elections were not going to be held and that the world was coming to accept a divided Vietnam as permanent. On January 21, 1957, even the Soviet Union had suggested that both South and North Vietnam be admitted to the United Nations. Finally, the Communist party of North Vietnam faced the danger of losing control over its southern arm, the Viet Cong; it could not afford to appear less resolute than the indigenous guerrillas, not if it expected to lead Vietnam's revolutionary forces.

As a result, a decision was made in Hanoi in late 1958 or early 1959 to take complete command of the military insurgency in the south and to squeeze the government of Diem as hard as it could. For the first time, the CIA found evidence of large-scale northern infiltration into the south. The war entered a new phase. Within a few months, armed insurgents appeared throughout the countryside. The Viet Cong grew bolder and more successful. The response was more repression by the Diem regime. This was the situation which confronted John F. Kennedy when he came to the White House in 1961. By any standard of measurement, his administration fell far short of dealing wisely with this inherited tragedy.

The first failure of Kennedy was that he neglected to reexamine the premises upon which U.S. military and political commitments to South Vietnam were based. The failure is inexplicable. Both the President and his vice president, Lyndon B. Johnson, had earlier expressed doubts about the Eisenhower administration's policy toward Vietnam. The reluctance of Lyndon Johnson, then Senate majority leader, to go along with intervention in 1954 had been a major factor in Eisenhower's decision to keep out. The foreign policy advisers of the new President were no admirers of the rigid policies of John Foster Dulles or his successors. And yet, the U.S. role in South Vietnam was not subject to any thorough reevaluation in 1961.

In those early days of the Kennedy administration, not Vietnam but Laos had the attention of Washington. Eisenhower had warned the incoming President, in the strongest terms, about the military and political situation in Laos. There was a sense in Washington that the Laotian struggle was going badly from the point of view of the United States, and that intervention might be required to forestay a Communist take-over. Eisenhower and those around him viewed the collapse of Laos as far more likely than a take-over in South Vietnam. But to most of the influential foreign-policy makers in the Kennedy administration, fighting the Communists in Laos would entail very difficult logistics and supply problems, and so they looked to a diplomatic compromise. These same policy makers, however, foresaw no insurmountable barriers to fighting in Vietnam. The key to victory was counterinsurgency. The bright young men who came with Kennedy in the early sixties thoroughly believed that under the proper conditions, guerrilla forces could be defeated by better-equipped guerrilla forces, that superior technique and weaponry and concepts of "nation-building" were an effective substitute for the old-fashioned use of massive armies to deal with local uprisings. The "green berets" were dashing, adventurous, Kennedyish, offering the prospect of unlimited gains for a limited expenditure of men and money. In one sense, Vietnam seemed an ideal proving ground for the theory of limited warfare.

Accordingly, Kennedy followed Eisenhower's lead in offering military aid to Diem and upped the commitment. In May 1961, the President ordered four hundred special forces and a hundred other military advisers into South Vietnam, raising the number of American armed personnel in the country above the number permissible under the terms of the Geneva agreements.* In September, more American military "advisers" were sent for the stated purpose of training Vietnamese soldiers. But they were also, of course, in the field with these soldiers. Again, an American President had sent men into a combat situation without authorization from Congress.

The Kennedy administration was moving along an uncharted course, with no overview of where it was headed or what it thought it could accomplish in South Vietnam, or why it needed to be accomplished. Nor had it any realistic estimate of what cost it would be willing to pay. The President's advisers themselves were of divided mind. Some analysts reported progress in Vietnam; others contended the opposite. Some believed that President Diem was the best hope for a stable government in the south; others argued that Diem was becoming increasingly unpopular and ought to be replaced so that the United States would not be saddled with a loser. Some mili-

---

* Under the terms of the Geneva agreements, the United States and other nonparticipants in the French-Vietnamese war were allowed to station military personnel in Vietnam only up to the number of their armed forces personnel in residence in Vietnam on the date the agreement was signed.

tary advisers believed that a few more American troops could turn the tide; others, even in 1961, thought that a large commitment of force would be needed to win. Vietnam was studied and restudied, while all the time people hoped that somehow, small incremental steps might obviate the need for a great leap forward into war.

For a time in 1962, the absence of any clear-cut, long-range policy in Washington seemed to have no negative effect on events in Vietnam. Most of the President's advisers believed that gains were being made against the Communist insurgency. Contingency plans were drawn up in the Pentagon for the withdrawal of all American military forces. A public statement was made that the United States would be entirely out of Vietnam by 1965.

In 1963 the bubble of optimism burst. South Vietnam's Buddhists—charging that President Diem was restricting their traditional rights and privileges —turned against him. Diem, a Catholic, responded with harsh countermeasures. World opinion was shocked by the sight of Buddhist self-immolations in the streets of Saigon. Diem's brother and sister-in-law, the Nhus, were reputed to favor an increasingly autocratic form of rule. Allegations of corruptions were widespread. The thinness of Diem's hold on the South Vietnam population became apparent. The country was coming apart.

The Kennedy administration was nevertheless unprepared to choose between alternatives then available to it. To some of Kennedy's advisers, Diem was a strong plus and should be supported whatever his faults; in their judgment, Diem's opponents were not religious but political, were allied with the Communists and should be treated as the enemy. Others thought Diem should be replaced by a more popular leader. Still others held to the notion that the United States could force Diem to carry out social reforms which would win him greater popularity and thus consolidate his control.

In public, Kennedy supported Diem. In private, the administration began selectively to cut off aid to Diem, hoping this would oblige him to curtail the powers of his brother and sister-in-law and reform his government. The administration also encouraged anti-Diem generals, who needed little else, to begin turning amorphous hopes for a coup into concrete plans. The outcome of this bits-and-pieces strategy could not have been worse. And when the anti-Diem generals did overthrow the South Vietnamese President in November 1963, the United States government had no settled response. Washington was almost as baffled as Saigon as to what to do next. With Diem dead, the military, political, and economic chaos spread. Most of the Vietnamese with technical competence and experience were purged from the Saigon government. The anti-Diem generals, quite naturally, looked to Washington to lend stability to the situation. And at this critical moment, President Kennedy was assassinated and Lyndon Baines Johnson took office.

When the Kennedy administration came to an end in late 1963, the range of American options was narrower than it had been in 1961. Sixteen thousand servicemen were in South Vietnam, about fifteen times the manpower commitment of 1961. There was no single, controlling political force in South Vietnam. The anti-Communists who replaced Diem were relatively weak and inexperienced and divided by intense jealousies. The Communist insurgency was more extensive than it had been two years before.

President Kennedy's failure to carefully define American objectives and realistically estimate the precise cost of achieving them was not a legacy from which Lyndon Johnson could easily profit. Perhaps the new President, too, should have begun by reexamining the entire Vietnamese problem. But a full-scale review was more difficult to conduct in 1963 than it would have been in 1961. Too many moves had been made; events were moving faster; the political stakes were higher. Two years earlier, the United States had the chance to choose whether and to what extent it would be responsible for the governing of South Vietnam. By 1963, the alternatives appeared to boil down to two: winning or losing a fairly major war.

Lyndon Johnson entered the White House with the firm intention of rallying a shaken nation. He was not disposed to rethink the conclusions of various Kennedy administration officials, all of whom he had asked to stay on. He would dedicate himself to carrying forward the policies of his predecessor. He was not in any frame of mind to search for fundamental errors of judgment made before his time. His first decision was made the day after the assassination, and it was essentially a reflex action.

On November 24, 1963, Henry Cabot Lodge, then ambassador to Vietnam, briefed the new President. It could not have been an encouraging report. The Saigon government was disabled, Viet Cong attacks had been stepped up in the wake of the anti-Diem coup and enemy guerrilla forces were now operating in large units with increasing effectiveness. The chief executive was told he had to bite the bullet. Johnson replied: "I am not going to be the President who saw Southeast Asia go the way China went." Communism would be stopped in Vietnam. No doubt the President believed that he was honoring a Kennedy commitment. Yet during those first confusing days of presidential succession, he was making a decision which his predecessor had held back from, and in so doing, Johnson wiped out whatever limited choices Kennedy may have thought remained. He nailed the American flag to Saigon's mast and there it stayed. In a New Year's message to General Duong Van Minh—President Diem's successor—Johnson stated:

> The United States will continue to furnish you and your people with the fullest measure of support in this bitter fight. We shall maintain in Vietnam American personnel and material as needed to assist you in achieving victory.

The level of economic aid and military assistance was again raised, though by 1964 nothing the U.S. could supply in the way of dollars and material seemed sufficient to break the back of the Communist guerrillas. The President was therefore receptive to other approaches. One of these was that the war could be won only if it were waged directly against Ho Chi Minh. This approach, attributed to presidential adviser W. W. Rostow, held that North Vietnam was no longer peripheral, that it had an industrial base to protect, and that a conventional war threat to its industrial facilities would bring it to the bargaining table. Covert military operations against the north were authorized by February 1964. This, as the authors of the famous Pentagon Papers were to note, was the "passing of a firebreak," since it was the first military action undertaken solely under the responsibility of the U.S. military command in South Vietnam. None of this was known to the American people; indeed, it was denied by the administration. Consequently, no theory was advanced or demanded to explain how this step could be constitutionally justified by the President.

Carrying the war to the north quite evidently opened the possibility of heavy bombing of military and industrial sites. But any such sustained policy would have to have some sort of congressional authorization. So although the administration had not been disturbed by the constitutional implications of covert, offensive measures against North Vietnam, it was nervous about an open offensive that did not have congressional approval.

Drafts of proposed authorizations were worked over during the summer months of 1964 by the State Department and the President's White House advisers, and were modeled on the Taiwan and Middle East resolutions. Since he was running for reelection that year, however, the President did not care to expose himself to the questions that would be asked if such a resolution were submitted. He therefore held it back. He did not hold back on aiding our Vietnamese allies, incrementally—and surreptitiously. In South Vietnam, the number of United States military personnel went up, economic aid multiplied, and a greater role in South Vietnamese politics was assumed by U.S. advisers in Saigon. Hostile actions against the north also increased. Air reconnaissance flights, retaliatory raids, and clandestine strikes were stepped up along with aid.

Finally, in August 1964, in what has become known as the Tonkin Gulf incident, two American destroyers were attacked by North Vietnamese torpedo boats in the Gulf of Tonkin. President Johnson immediately sent U.S. planes on a large-scale bombing raid of North Vietnam and followed this by sending Congress the draft of a resolution to legitimize such acts as the one he had already taken.* The President's statement put the case against the North Vietnamese in dramatic terms. Thus, it was in an atmosphere of rather contrived urgency that the resolution reached Congress and was introduced by Senator William Fulbright, chairman of the Senate Foreign Relations Committee, and by Representative Thomas Morgan. The resolution read in part:

> *Resolved by the Senate and the House of Representatives of the United States of America in Congress assembled,* That the Congress approves and supports the determination of the President, as Commander in Chief, to take all necessary measures to repel any armed attack against the forces of the United States and to prevent further aggression.

The resolution placed Congress on record as declaring that safeguarding the peace and security of Southeast Asia was in the national interest of the

---

* There has been considerable conjecture as to whether the Tonkin Gulf attack was not initiated by the North Vietnamese as a reprisal for undercover raids that the South Vietnamese were then conducting in that area against the territory of North Vietnam. There has also been speculation that the attacks were not accurately reported by the administration. Later reviews of the events of August 1964 suggest the conjecture had some factual support. Interesting as these historical arguments may be, however, they do not change one fact. In August 1964, Congress had no alternative but to believe the truth of the administration's report of Tonkin Gulf hostilities and to base its actions on that report.

United States, and that "the United States is, therefore, prepared, as the President determines, to take
all necessary steps, including the use of armed force,
to assist any member or protocol state of the Southeast Asia Collective Defense Treaty requesting assistance in defense of its freedom." The powers to be
granted to the President were to expire only when
"the President shall determine that the peace and security of the area is reasonably assured," or when the
Congress had rescinded the resolution by concurrent
resolution. It passed the Senate with only two nay
votes, and it passed the House unanimously. Congress was praised by the press for the speed with
which it responded to the President's request and the
sense of responsibility it had shown in doing so.

What the Congress had done was to hand the President a blank check to conduct a major war. Having
full knowledge of the presidential powers it was authorizing, Congress refused to believe that Lyndon
Johnson would use all the powers given him. The
following exchange between Senator Daniel Brew-
ster of Maryland and Senator Fulbright is illustrative:

> MR. BREWSTER. I had the opportunity to see warfare
> not so very far from this area, and it was very mean. I
> would look with great dismay on a situation involving
> the landing of large land armies on the continent of
> Asia. So my question is whether there is anything in
> the resolution which would authorize or recommend
> or approve the landing of large American armies in
> Vietnam or in China.
> MR. FULBRIGHT. There is nothing in the resolution,
> as I read it, that contemplates it. I agree with the Sen-
> ator that that is the last thing we would want to do.
> *However, the language of the resolution would not*
> *prevent it. It would authorize whatever the Com-*

mander in Chief feels is necessary. It does not restrain the Executive from doing it. Whether or not that should ever be done is a matter of wisdom under the circumstances that exist at the particular time it is contemplated. This kind of question should more properly be addressed to the chairman of the Armed Services Committee. Speaking for my own committee, everyone I have heard has said that the last thing we want to do is to become involved in a land war in Asia; that our power is sea and air, and that this is what we hope will deter the Chinese Communists and the North Vietnamese from spreading the war. That is what is contemplated. *The resolution does not prohibit that, or any other kind of activity.* (Emphasis added.)

Senator Fulbright repeated the point in an exchange with Senator John Sherman Cooper of Kentucky.

MR. COOPER. . . . Does the Senator consider that in enacting this resolution we are satisfying that requirement of article IV of the Southeast Asia Collective Defense Treaty? In other words, are we now giving the President advance authority to take whatever action he may deem necessary respecting South Vietnam and its defense, or with respect to the defense of any other country included in the treaty?

MR. FULBRIGHT. I think that is correct.

MR. COOPER. *Then, looking ahead, if the President decided that it was necessary to use such force as could lead into war, we will give that authority by this resolution?*

MR. FULBRIGHT. *That is the way I would interpret it.* If a situation later developed in which we thought the approval should be withdrawn, it could be withdrawn by concurrent resolution. That is the reason for the third section. (Emphasis added.)

President Johnson expressed his appreciation for Congress' speedy action, and within six months the United States was engaged in the all-out bombing of North Vietnam. Within nine months, the United States was fighting a large-scale land war in South Vietnam.

Any reading of the Tonkin Gulf debate will reveal the tendency on the part of members of Congress to assume that in military matters the President is more likely to be right than anyone else. Senator after senator and representative after representative took the floor to criticize past Vietnamese policy, urge that no large military moves be made in Asia, caution against antagonizing Communist China, and then announce that he supported a resolution which empowered the President to do whatever he thought had to be done. Why not surrender congressional war powers, if it meant they would not have to be used? But the powers given the President *were* used. And we were not nearer to answering the basic question: how does Congress regain its constitutional prerogatives after three decades of unchallenged presidential usurpation of warmaking authority?

Part II

7

Forcing Disengagement

Tonkin should have sounded the alarm to the public; it didn't. The country was not agitated by the prospect of a police action to put down communism and thereby in some fashion "honor" a "commitment" which somehow had been made sometime by the U.S. government. Protest grew slowly out of a small, largely academically oriented movement relying largely upon peaceful means to register its dissent. Those who joined the university teach-ins and youthful peace marches knew they were a minority and sought to educate the country. If antiwar pressures could threaten a President's political base, he would be forced to change his policy. Initially that was roughly the attitude of members of Congress also, at least those of them who were skeptical or downright opposed to our deepening involvement. They would try and persuade the President to shift into reverse. Implicitly, these critics accepted the supposition expressed by Nicholas Katzenbach, then undersecretary of state, to the Senate Foreign Relations Committee in 1967: the President has preeminent authority to direct our foreign and military policies; the legislators were outsiders. So the insiders announced what would be done and did it: the outsiders observed and from time to time sought to advise or cajole or warn.

Some sought to move the President by using the lever of the legislature's power to investigate, hoping that public hearings on the war would educate the public to its government's waywardness. This strategy was as rational as it was ineffective. No hearings could compete in authoritativeness or drama with the President's presentation to a national audience. He, not they, was commander in chief. Secretaries of state and secretaries of defense regularly appeared on the Hill. The questioning got tougher, and Congress was occasionally infuriated by official evasiveness.

When it became obvious that the dogged effort of Senator Fulbright to change policy through congressional hearings was doomed, other legislators—notably Senators Eugene McCarthy and Robert Kennedy—resolved to challenge the President head on. If only the President could end the war, and the present chief executive would not do it, then a new President must be elected. Their challenge was unexpectedly but only partially, successful. Lyndon Johnson chose not to stand for reelection in 1968. In effect, he was driven from office, but his policy was not. True, the new President, Richard M. Nixon, had said he had a "secret" plan to end the war. But as events soon showed, the plan of 1968 was as ephemeral as most campaign speeches. The war went on full blast, and congressmen who opposed it were obliged to reexamine their strategies. If changing Presidents was not the key to changing presidential policies, then perhaps they were looking at the wrong branch of the federal government for change. Perhaps the legislature would and could now legislate an end to this undeclared war against North Vietnam and its guerrilla arm, the Viet Cong.

By approving the Gulf of Tonkin Resolution in 1964, Congress had offered to pay for the trip without asking how long it would take, where it would end, or whether it was necessary. The executive branch had been authorized to conduct a major war in Southeast Asia to preserve the independence of South Vietnam. No matter how unwise Congress may have been in giving an openended grant of authority to the executive branch to deal with the Vietnam situation, Congress was exercising its constitutional prerogative to decide how and under what conditions American armed forces would be committed to hostilities. When Lyndon Johnson, in 1965 and thereafter, decided to boost the U.S. contribution, he did so not against the expressed wish of the Congress, but with it. And when Richard Nixon chose to interpret the 1968 election as a mandate to deal with Indochina very largely as he wished, he too was operating within boundaries of authority set by the Congress in the Gulf of Tonkin Resolution.

Those who after 1968 sought to limit or halt U.S. participation in the war by legislation quickly discovered that they were confronted with serious legal as well as political problems. From a legal standpoint, the Constitution provides that a war once authorized by Congress shall be conducted by the President acting as commander in chief. The Congress is not empowered to make battlefield decisions; it cannot and should not attempt to order specific military advances or withdrawals. Legal limitations are reinforced by political realities. A nation at war expects decisions regarding the course of that conflict to be made by one man. It tends to look with suspicion on legislative bodies which believe that they possess more knowledge and insight than the man who has been elected to guide the country through day-by-day downturns and even crises. It also expects that America's fighting men will hear only one voice emanating from the councils of government as they strive to reach difficult objectives through dangerous military means.

On the other hand, the Founding Fathers clearly did intend that Congress play a role after a war had begun. The Constitution requires Congress to review military appropriations at least every two years in order to guard against "the keeping of troops without evident necessity." Since Congress must vote funds to support the armed forces and can make rules to regulate those forces, it can also refuse to vote funds or vote them subject to certain conditions. The checks and balances system requires that, however trying the circumstances, the legislative branch must be prepared to restrict an abuse of power by a strong-willed chief executive.

For those in Congress who accepted this overseer responsibility, who believed that the United States was on a deadend course in Vietnam, the question was how to exercise the oversight function. At least four different answers were put forward, and each was studied and tried, with differing degrees of success.

If the legislative branch wanted to stay off a collision course with the executive branch, its least provocative response was a simple statement of policy it wished the government to follow, no sanctions attached. On two occasions during 1971, Congress did declare that our objective should be to terminate "at the earliest practicable date" U.S. military operations in Indochina. The President was urged to set a date by which all our forces would be withdrawn, contingent only on the release of American prisoners of war and an accounting for Americans missing in action. Congress further called on the President to negotiate an immediate cease-fire with the North Vietnamese government and to establish, through negotiations, a phased withdrawal of our forces from Indochina in return for a phased release of our POWs. On both occasions, the legislators were rebuffed: they did "not represent the policies of this [the Nixon] Administration." And since the legislative requests had no sanctions, they could be ignored. In the most stark terms, a Congress that wanted to change fundamental national policy and at the same time avoid a collision with the President, would be told to mind its own business.

The second legislative option was an indirect attack on the chief executive's conduct of the war. Most members of Congress believed that the legislative branch was empowered to define the extent of the authorization it had given through the Gulf of Tonkin Resolution. Congress could, therefore, by conditioning its military appropriations, restrict the movement of U.S. troops across recognized national boundaries. Although there were no precedents for such legislative restrictions imposed during a war, Congress had in the past curtailed presidential use of the armed forces. In 1909, it had ordered President Taft not to spend appropriations for the Marine Corps, unless Marine officers and enlisted men were stationed on naval vessels. In 1940, Congress mandated that men drafted into the armed forces should not be sent outside the Western Hemisphere, except in the territories and possessions of the United States. Working from these precedents, Senator John Sherman Cooper, a Republican from Kentucky, and Senator Frank Church, a Democrat from Idaho, sponsored a measure in 1969 to prohibit the expenditure of appropriated funds to support American ground troops in Laos and Thailand. The Senate incorporated their proposal into the defense appropriations bill of December 15, 1969, by a vote of 73–17, and the House of Representatives went along.

Unfortunately, the Congress had picked the wrong countries. In the guise of "winding down the war" President Nixon on April 29, 1970, sent American and South Vietnamese troops into Cambodia to "clean out major enemy sanctuaries" and capture COSVN, the purported Communist headquarters directing all enemy activities in South Vietnam.

To many of us, the invasion of Cambodia was not only a military and political blunder, but a slap at Congress, which had repeatedly and both formally and informally urged that our military operations at least be limited to South Vietnam. A renewed campaign was mounted, again by Senators Cooper and Church, to extend the prohibition on U.S. ground troops to include Cambodia as well as Laos and Thailand. At this point the administration dug in its heels, charging that Congress was infringing the President's powers as commander in chief to defend American forces in the field. The White House argued that the invasion had been a tactical necessity, and that it was limited in scope and duration. The President said that all American troops would be withdrawn from Cambodia by July 1, 1970.

Supporters of the Cooper-Church initiative denied that Congress was trying to decide tactical questions in setting geographical limits beyond which the President could not exercise his constitutional right of command. They insisted Congress had always had the right to say where U.S. military forces could and could not be engaged.

The relevance of these arguments to the Constitution was somewhat more ambiguous than either side was willing to concede. I had no doubt that in peacetime Congress could prohibit the President from sending American troops into any particular country. But once our armed forces were fighting, it seemed to me an altogether different situation. Under those circumstances, Congress could still delineate geographical boundaries for hostilities in which American troops would be engaged—even if those boundaries had already been exceeded by the time of the legislative initiative. However, the congressional imposition was not absolute. For example, Congress could not constitutionally prevent the commander in chief from ordering the hot pursuit of fleeing enemy troops across geographical boundaries, when that pursuit was necessary to repel an attack upon, or terminate a battle with, American forces. Neither could Congress abrogate the right of a commander in chief in time of war to order an attack across national boundary lines, if the purpose was clearly "preemptive"; that is to avoid imminent attack on American troops by enemy forces stationed in that foreign country.

Nevertheless, I had no difficulty supporting the Cooper-Church initiative. Nor did I see any constitutional problem in the immediate enforcement of its provisions. American troops had been ordered into Cambodia not to pursue fleeing enemy troops or, in my judgment, to forestall a clear and present danger of imminent attack on American forces. Even if a case could have been made that the President's April 29 decision to invade neutral Cambodia had been to prevent an imminent enemy attack, there was still no justification for a two-month military operation whose stated purpose was to search for and destroy enemy troops and supplies.

The debate on Cooper-Church did not proceed as I had hoped it would. Antiwar sentiment in the country had been enflamed by the attack in Cambodia, and in consequence many members of Congress took the floor to make broad and, in some cases, unsupportable assertions regarding presidential and congressional warmaking power. By the time passions had cooled somewhat, passage of the Cooper-Church initiative appeared possible only if its language specifically exempted American troops already in Cambodia. Reluctantly, I acceded to this position—troubled by the failure of Congress to rap the President's wrists harder for his unwarranted invasion, but even more so by the failure of many of my colleagues to recognize the dangerous implications of their defense of unilateral presidential prerogatives.

But if I felt frustrated by that debate, I soon saw that it was only a prelude to more frustration and confusion. For as Congress began to explore its third legislative option, namely, cutting off funds for U.S. military activities, it became evident that many legislators misconceived the Constitution's delineation of the warmaking powers. There was a growing body of opinion—not only within the executive branch but in the Congress—that was ready to tolerate almost no limitation on presidential power.

In briefly reviewing the history of these congressional initiatives, we may start with the proposals of Republican Senator Charles Goodell of New York. In the latter part of 1969, Goodell—who had been appointed by Governor Nelson Rockefeller to fill out the term of Robert Kennedy—opened fire on the Nixon administration for having no viable plan for peace. This being so, he said, Congress should assert its will and force an end to the war. Goodell proposed that "all American military personnel be withdrawn from Vietnam on or before December 1, 1970; so that the retention even of noncombat military training personnel after that date . . . [will] not be permitted without the enactment by Congress of further legislation specifically approving such retention." No appropriated funds could be used after December 1, 1970, to maintain American military forces in Vietnam.

The Goodell bill was not taken very seriously at the time of its introduction. Most members of Congress thought the senator from New York did not accurately reflect the temper of the country and that any legislator who joined with him was in danger of being shot down politically. Moreover, it was widely believed, even by members who were strongly antiwar, that the President had managed to defuse Vietnam as a political issue. Perhaps, as Goodell charged, the administration had no overall plan for peace, nevertheless the President was withdrawing American troops and cutting back on war expenditures. Under those conditions, most congressmen chose to avoid an eyeball-to-eyeball confrontation with the commander in chief.

But with the invasion of Cambodia in the spring of 1970, the mood altered dramatically. Congressmen who opposed the war sensed that if the President were left to his own devices, the conflict would continue throughout at least his first four-year term. In the wake of the invasion, more legislators began to look with favor on proposals which had seemed to them too extreme only a few months before. On the day the President announced that American troops had entered Cambodia, Senator George McGovern of South Dakota and Republican Senator Mark Hatfield of Oregon called for an end to hostilities by a date certain and threatened the curtailment of financial support for the war after that date. Other end-the-war proposals surfaced, most of them derivations or modifications of the Goodell-McGovern-Hatfield initiatives.

During the summer and fall of 1970, literally thousands of speeches were made and articles written on the advantages and disadvantages of congressional assertions of power to disengage the United States from the war. Those who followed the long, often tedious debates knew that the antiwar measures were doomed to defeat. But to those who either favored or opposed them, the number of votes that could be gathered for their passage seemed important, for the number reflected in some measure the shifts in public opinion. In September 1970, when a revised McGovern-Hatfield proposal finally came to a vote, thirty-nine senators favored its enactment—a new high. And from that day on congressional support for some type of end-the-war legislation rose steadily.

By 1972, a majority of the Senate and a near majority of the House of Representatives favored some legislation terminating hostilities by a date certain—if the enemy would first return America's prisoners of war and provide information on those listed as missing in action. Yet Congress was not able, over administration objection, to enact any bill forcing an end to U.S. military action. Worse, from a long-range institutional standpoint, was the tenor of many of the congressional debates. At various times, opponents and even proponents of end-the-war legislation either argued for, or assumed, some odd constitutional notions. Thus, during early debates on the McGovern-Hatfield proposal, it was not unusual to hear members asserting that the President had the broadest power to commit troops to hostilities in situations he believed threatened the security of this nation or its allies. Other of my colleagues claimed presidential power to protect American troops or citizens or property under virtually any circumstance. The debates which were intended in part to produce legislation limiting presidential power often produced wild claims that the Constitution could be turned on its head and that no legislative restraints on the executive branch could be properly imposed.

When the Nixon administration decided during the summer of 1970 to repeal the Gulf of Tonkin Resolution, war critics were taken by surprise. If that resolution was the source of the war's constitutional legitimacy, then its repeal should signal an immediate termination of the war—consistent only with the orderly withdrawal of American forces. But Senator Robert Dole of Kansas, the administration's chief spokesman during the debate on repeal of Tonkin, did not see it this way. Dole argued that the commander in chief did not need that resolution's authorization to conduct hostilities in Vietnam, since these hostilities were now connected with a planned, phased troop withdrawal, and the power of the President to protect troops was his by virtue of his constitutional power as commander in chief. Whether the troops were on the offense or defense made no difference; neither did the duration of their presence in Vietnam: Congress had originally authorized their use and the President had pledged their eventual removal.

I engaged Senator Dole in a colloquy on the Senate floor on June 23, 1970, in order to explore the implications of this theory of executive power. I asked whether the President, acting as commander in chief to protect American fighting men in Vietnam, could conduct a preemptive strike against China to wipe out "sanctuaries" without any authorization from, or consultation with, Congress. Senator Dole replied, "It is not required."

> MR. EAGLETON. It is not required. So it is the thought of the Senator that as Commander in Chief, with no Gulf of Tonkin Resolution, the President could have an air strike in Red China?
> MR. DOLE. This is right. I assume so. . . .

That answer and various other statements of administration spokesmen posed an awkward question. On the one hand, if the Tonkin Gulf Resolution was repealed and the war went on, a very dangerous precedent would be established. It might be argued, for example, that once Congress authorized hostilities, a simple repeal of that authorization could not limit presidential power to continue military activities so long as he claimed to be winding them down.

On the other hand, I was influenced by the argument that repeal would demonstrate disapproval of the Vietnam War and at least imply regret that the original authorization had ever been granted. And it seemed to me that the risks in repeal could be minimized if repeal were coupled with either passage of the McGovern-Hatfield bill or some similar proposal, or passage of legislation—albeit with some reservations—clarifying presidential war powers. Accordingly, I voted repeal; it passed the Senate by a vote of 81–10 and was adopted by the House-Senate conference committee. But having voted for repeal, I was now obliged to do what I could to reassert the constitutional rights of Congress.

Of course I was not alone. Although there were differences on the best way of reaching the goal, a number of members of both political parties were ready to reexamine the balance of warmaking power between the executive and legislative branches. After the Senate debate on the repeal of the Tonkin resolution, Senator Barry Goldwater of Arizona noted on June 23, 1970:

> I have come to the conclusion . . . that we would be better off discussing two constitutional amendments; one to better describe and prescribe the powers of Congress in the area of warmaking, and a second to describe and prescribe, if we have to, the powers of the President; because until we do either, I think we are going to go on with a very misunderstood idea of what the Constitution gives to both Congress and the President as powers.

In the House of Representatives, Clement Zablocki of Pennsylvania was the first to act. On August 13, 1970, he introduced a joint resolution expressing the sense of the Congress that, "whenever feasible" the President should seek appropriate congressional consultations before involving the armed forces of the United States in armed conflict, and should "continue such consultation periodically during such armed conflict." This vaguely worded resolution fell far short of delineating the authority of the President and the Congress to make war and indeed allowed Congress far less responsibility than did the Constitution.

Republican Senator Jacob Javits of New York opened the battle on the Senate side, introducing in June 1970 a war powers bill slightly stronger than Zablocki's but nonetheless skirting many of the fundamental issues.

The Javits bill coupled a general outline of the President's emergency powers with a requirement that the chief executive report to Congress if those powers were used.

Both proposals in effect realigned the constitutional balance by putting Congress in the position of either ratifying or rejecting hostilities initiated unilaterally by the President, rather than in the position of making the precedent decision of whether those hostilities should ever begin. Moreover, they tended to rely upon the same vague terms—such as "protecting" American troops or civilians or property or undertaking "hostilities"—which had already been subject to varying, inconsistent and dangerous interpretations. As I saw it, Congress had to lay down the basic guidelines for restoring joint congressional and presidential responsibility for any commitment of U.S. forces to hostilities abroad. At the same time, the Congress had to allow the President sufficient discretion to take emergency action to meet attacks on the United States and its forces and to rescue American civilians under siege abroad. A balance would have to be struck, but the balance would have to rest upon the premise that the constitutional separation between the power to initiate and the power to conduct hostilities was valid.

Senate Joint Resolution 59 which I introduced on March 1, 1971, made four major points:

First, it required that in virtually all cases involving the initiation of hostilities between United States forces and foreign military forces, the President would not act without prior authorization from Congress. No treaty commitment was to be regarded as self-enforcing, and if American armed forces were used in support of one of this country's allies, Congress must specifically authorize that use. An authorization could not be inferred from such indirect legislative actions as the passage of appropriations bills. The resolution, in addition, provided that the term "hostilities" covered land, air and naval actions and encompassed situations where the deployment of troops abroad could reasonably be expected to lead to immediate hostilities, or where American forces were being used as advisers to the troops of a foreign nation engaged in hostilities.

Second, it recognized that Congress could authorize hostilities through either a declaration of war, a statute, or a joint resolution. Such authorization could define the extent of the hostilities, thus confining the U.S. combat role to certain specified areas.

Third, the resolution provided that once hostilities had begun, the President could order U.S. forces into a country with which the United States is not engaged in hostilities only:

> (a) when in hot pursuit of fleeing enemy forces who have attacked, or engaged in battle with, the Armed Forces of the United States and then retreated to the territory or airspace of such country, to the extent necessary to repel such attack or complete such battle, or
> (b) when a clear and present danger exists of an imminent attack on the United States or the Armed

Forces of the United States by enemy troops located in such country, to the extent necessary to eliminate such danger.

Fourth, the resolution granted the President's authority in three instances to commit the armed forces of the United States to hostilities in the absence of congressional authorization: (1) an attack upon the United States, (2) an attack upon United States forces, and (3) the protection of American citizens abroad who were under attack because they were American citizens. In line with historical precedents, the resolution allowed the President wide latitude in situations falling under the first category and a narrow range of choices for situations falling in the third category. Thus, in the first category, the President was authorized to

repel an attack on the United States by military forces with whom the United States is not engaged in hostilities at the time of such attack and to eliminate or reduce the effectiveness of any future attacks by such military forces which are committing the attack being repelled. . . .

In the second category, he was empowered to

repel an attack on the Armed Forces of the United States by military forces with whom the United States is not engaged in hostilities at the time of such attack and concurrently to eliminate or reduce any clear and present danger of future attacks by the military forces which are committing the attack being repelled. . . .

In the third category, he was authorized to

withdraw citizens of the United States, as rapidly as possible, from any country in which such citizens, there due to their own volition and with the express or tacit consent of the government of such country, are being subjected to an imminent threat to their lives, either sponsored by such government or beyond the power of such government to control: *Provided,* That the President shall make every effort to terminate such a threat without using the Armed Forces of the United States; *And provided further,* That the President shall, where possible, obtain the consent of the government of such country before using the Armed Forces of the United States.

In all three instances, however, the President would be required to report to Congress promptly, and Congress would have to decide within thirty days from the date on which hostilities were initiated whether these presidentially initiated hostilities were to continue or to end.

The resolution was not intended as the final answer. There were many tangled problems which needed close scrutiny by Congress and the President. Nevertheless, I believed that my resolution was more restrictive of unilateral presidential power than any that had been introduced to date.

8

Moving Toward a Vote

By early 1966, State Department officials had not one but five separate legal justifications for what was being done by the United States in Vietnam. First, the department argued that Congress, by virtue of the Gulf of Tonkin Resolution had sanctioned presidential action. Second, the department contended that even if the resolution had not validly authorized American participation in the war, Congress had done so through a series of defense appropriations acts which served as "endorsement" and "approval" of the administration's actions. Moreover, it contended that when Congress ratified the Southeast Asian Collective Defense Treaty and the President signed it, a blank check was given to him as commander in chief, to be filled in as he chose, whenever he deemed it necessary to aid in the defense of the signatories of the treaty, or other nations covered by that treaty. That this agreement—as well as all other collective defense treaties signed by the United States—stated that each nation would meet collective dangers "in accordance with its constitutional processes" did not, argued the State Department, oblige the President to wait upon the advice or consent of Congress in any particular case.

This theory was accompanied by a fourth contention, based on "precedent" and "practice," that since previous Presidents had committed American troops to certain military activities without clear-cut congressional authorization, then the commitment in Indochina must be permissible.* Finally, the State Department suggested that perhaps the Constitution had been misconstrued by the war critics. The correct interpretation, according to the Johnson administration, was that the executive branch had the "power to deploy American forces abroad and commit them to military operations when the President deems such action necessary to maintain the security and defense of the United States."

As a lawyer, I found four of these five theories absurd. I agreed that the Tonkin Gulf Resolution had authorized participation in the Vietnam War, but I could not accept the idea that broad appropriations acts authorizing money for a large number of vital governmental functions could be read as specific authorizations for hostilities. Neither could I agree with the concept of self-executing treaties. When these treaties decreed that "constitutional processes" would be observed, it seemed to me to mean that a decision to defend one of our allies would have to be made by Congress. As for the argument of "precedent," I had read enough American history to know that warmaking by the executive on his own had been the exception, not the rule.

---

* This theory became known as the "bank robber" proposition: if a number of bank robbers proved successful, the act of bank robbery would have to be legalized.

But I must add that none of these three theories troubled me, for each could be handily dealt with by the Congress. Appropriations acts could always be couched in terms which would prevent their being read as authorizations. If necessary, Congress could limit the effect of previous treaties by passage of a clarifying statute, and it could circumscribe the application of any future treaties by adding more limiting language to them. Congress could also point out inconsistencies in warmaking precedents through hearings and could urge the President to avoid senseless attempts to claim that the Constitution's provisions could ever be altered by previous practice.

On the other hand, I viewed with deep apprehension the Johnson administration's claim of broad warmaking powers to defend our security. For that claim could only be based on a thorough constitutional revision, rendering the Founding Fathers' decision to give Congress the power "to declare war" virtually meaningless.

When Richard Nixon took office, I hoped for a more sensible, legally defensible policy. Nixon was unencumbered by any direct identification with or service to the failed policies of the past. And if he was truly a "strict constructionist," then surely he would not arrogate to himself sole power to use American forces to meet undefined national security threats. Once again, I was to be disappointed in a new President. Rather than deflating theories which maximized presidential power, he inflated them. In the view of the Nixon State Department, the President could act on his own wherever and whenever he deemed "the security interest of the United States" was at stake. And if our forces were committed to battle, the President could keep them fighting so long as he wished in order to "win a just peace." Soldiers, sailors, marines; tanks, guns, planes, missiles; indeed the whole might of the United States was to be played on the chessboard of world power politics—with Congress as observer of the game plan. This was the Nixon interpretation of "separation of powers" and it became manifest during the 1970 debates over the Cooper-Church proposal to place Cambodia off limits to American ground troops, the McGovern-Hatfield initiative to end the war, and the administration's effort to repeal the Tonkin Gulf Resolution.

My response was the introduction in March 1971, of Senate Joint Resolution 59, defining and delineating presidential warmaking powers. I knew full well the hurdles any such proposal would have to jump. I was a freshman senator and not a member of the Foreign Relations Committee to which the resolution would be referred. Even if my proposal somehow were to pass the Senate, I had few allies in the House of Representatives, and a substantial majority in that body had time and again proven its unwillingness to resist any presidental exercise of military power. Finally, even if some such proposal was enacted by Congress, it could be vetoed or the President could refuse to accept its dictates.

But even if the resolution did not pass, it might force candidates for national office to take a position on it and prompt the public to think about the respective roles of the executive and legislative branches. And if such a resolution was enacted and did escape a presidential veto, its impact could be enormous. Not only might it compel future Presidents to respect narrower constructions of executive power, but it could be the vehicle for returning various war power questions to the federal courts—which had been extremely leery about intervening in this political thicket.

As I went to the floor of the Senate to introduce my resolution, the stage for serious debate had been set. The Foreign Relations Committee opened its hearings on war powers on March 8, 1971. Before it were Senator Javits' bill, S. 731, and my joint resolution, S. J. Res. 59. It soon received two other bills, one from Senator Robert Taft of Ohio and another from Senator Lloyd Bentsen of Texas. Along with these came an outpouring of statements and testimony from the senator sponsors and from a host of organizations and expert witnesses. Hearings continued sporadically for several months, and by early May I had begun to doubt whether any consensus could be reached which would permit a strong war powers initiative to emerge from the Foreign Relations Committee.

Then on May 11, 1971, Senator John Stennis of Mississippi, the powerful chairman of the Senate Armed Services Committee, submitted his own war powers resolution (S. J. Res. 95). It was an event like the landing of American troops in Normandy in World War II! Stennis' proposal bore marked similarities to my own,* but it was introduced at the right time by the right man. In the Senate since 1947, Stennis was recognized as the leader of the Senate's southern conservative bloc and as an intelligent legislator

---

* The major deletion from the Stennis bill was the section of Senate Joint Resolution 59 which dealt with the powers of the President to invade third countries once hostilities between the United States and a defined enemy had begun. Senator Stennis believed that serious constitutional problems were raised by a legislative effort to restrict the President's commander-in-chief powers during hostilities. The senator and I still disagree on this point.

whose stands were well-reasoned, well-articulated. His influence was enormous. He was a consistent defender of U.S. policy on Vietnam. His introduction of a restrictive resolution was a strong indication, therefore, that not only those who opposed the Indochina conflict, but those who supported it as well, believed that the constitutional balance had to be redressed.

In the Senate as elsewhere, progress comes through compromise. By October 1971, Senator Javits and I had agreed to meld our two initiatives into a single bill. In November, Senator Stennis endorsed in principle a Javits-Eagleton draft, and in a letter of November 24 to Javits, Stennis declared that the new draft bill "represents a reasonable compromise and a good first effort toward drafting this difficult legislation." On March 29, 1972, the Foreign Relations Committee reported the compromise bill, S. 2956, to the floor of the Senate. We were on the move this time!

S. 2956 offered a precise definition of the constitutional authority of Congress and the President in the exercise of their respective powers in situations of undeclared war. It further set out to "insure that the collective judgment of both Congress and the President will apply" when American forces are committed to hostilities. The bill made plain that it was not intended to diminish the recognized power of the President to act in emergencies, but rather was meant to insure that Congress would be part and parcel of all decisions that could lead the United States into a major war.

To anticipate and take account of the exigencies of modern warfare and the complexities of international relations, Section 3 of the act codified those emergency situations in which the President could commit armed forces without specific authority of Congress. Thus, he could act

(1) to repel an attack upon the United States, its territories and possessions; to take necessary and appropriate retaliatory actions in the event of such an attack; and to forestall the direct and imminent threat of such an attack;

(2) to repel an armed attack against the Armed Forces of the United States located outside of the United States, its territories and possessions, and to forestall the direct and imminent threat of such an attack;

(3) to protect while evacuating citizens and nationals of the United States, as rapidly as possible, from any country in which such citizens and nationals are present, with the express or tacit consent of the government of such country and are being subjected to a direct and imminent threat to their lives, either sponsored by such government or beyond the power of such government to control: *Provided,* that the President shall make every effort to terminate such a threat without using the Armed Forces of the United States: *And provided further,* that the President shall where possible, obtain the consent of the government of such country before using the Armed Forces of the United States;

The fourth subsection of Section 3 was what Senator Javits called the "heart and core" of the legislation. This subsection obliged the President to seek the authority of Congress before committing U.S. forces to hostilities in all instances other than those "emergency situations" specified in the bill. The key phrase was "pursuant to specific statutory authorization." To explain those five words, a provision was inserted stating that no appropriation act or treaty could be construed as a "specific statutory authorization."

The thirty-day authorization period (Section 5 of the bill) guaranteed that Congress would retain its responsibilities even in emergency situations. Under that section, any presidential action, taken under the bill's carefully defined emergency provisions, could not "be sustained beyond 30 days from the date of the introduction of such armed forces in hostilities . . . unless the continued use thereof . . . has been authorized in specific legislation enacted for that purpose by the Congress. . . ."

Although the choice of thirty days was arbitrary, it was felt that it allowed both sufficient presidential flexibility and time for consultation between the executive and legislative branches. It assumed a definable point in time when an emergency action— repelling an attack—changes its nature and becomes retaliatory. At that point, a decision to go ahead or stop must be made, and that decision could only be made by the Congress. That was the premise of S. 2956.

When debate opened on the War Powers Act on March 29, Senate opponents presented a brief prepared by the Department of State which posed the central question: "[To] what extent the President has power to use the armed forces by virtue of his role as Commander-in-Chief, and in the conduct of foreign relations." The opposition formed behind predictable lines. Senators Barry Goldwater of Arizona and Peter Dominick of Colorado led the attack on the Republican side of the aisle, joined by Senator Gale McGee of Wyoming, a liberal Democrat who believed that the chief executive should have an undefined charter to defend America's best interests. All these men, Vietnam notwithstanding, held to the concept of a strong president relatively unshackled by legislative restrictions. In their judgment, S. 2956 was too severe and might handicap a president in an unpredictable and rapidly changing world. As a compromise, they favored nothing stronger in 1972 than a congressionally created commission to study the war powers issue.

The Goldwater-Dominick position was more ideological and was based on a broad reading of the Constitution's grant of powers to the President. With State Department assistance, Senator Goldwater had compiled a list of some 198 incidents in which American military forces had purportedly been employed abroad without congressional authorization. He and Senator Dominick stood on these precedents, and, following the administration's line, they argued that the exigencies of the modern era made mandatory a relatively unrestrained commander in chief.

As is often the case, the opening debate was little more than a sparring match, with each side attempting to measure the reach of the other. It was not until the limits of the debate had become more firmly established that statements and exchanges became more heated. At first, critics of S. 2956 centered on a provision in Section 3 requiring explicit congressional authorization "for the assignment of members of the Armed Forces . . . to command, coordinate, participate in the movement of, or accompany . . . the military forces of any foreign country . . . when such forces are engaged, or there exists an imminent threat that such forces will become engaged, in military hostilities." They charged that this provision would badly damage the unified command structure of the North Atlantic Treaty Organization and would hobble American commanders of NATO forces in the event of hostilities in Europe.

In response, supporters of the bill pointed out that the provision cited was not intended to affect the command structure of any of our defense alliances, but to assure that the assignment of "advisers" or other military aides to foreign governments would receive the prior approval of Congress. The purpose of the provision was to prevent a repetition of the Vietnam experience. But repeated assurances that the NATO unified command would in no way be endangered were unacceptable to Senator Goldwater.

Objection was also raised to the thirty-day provision of Section 5 which was thought to infringe on the commander in chief's responsibility to defend against attack either the United States or U.S. forces stationed abroad. The constitutional right of the President to repel such attacks, it was contended, could not be bound in any fashion by the Congress. Here, Goldwater and Dominick found a surprising ally in Senator John Sherman Cooper. Cooper was a loyal supporter of the bill, but he had reservations about the constitutionality of limiting the President's recognized power to repel attacks. He agreed that Congress must be brought into the picture at the outset if there was any chance of the nation's going to war. He also recognized that at some point, the repelling of an attack might go beyond self-defense. He was, therefore, in general agreement with the idea of placing a quantitative limit on the President's emergency powers, but he felt that the chief executive ought to be able to act defensively beyond thirty days.

The sponsors of S. 2956 replied that they had not sought to change the status of the President as commander in chief and could not do so under the Constitution. The President, they noted, would always have the right to defend American forces, even when they were being withdrawn as the result of a denial of further congressional authorization to continue their original objective. Nevertheless, some definition had to be made of a time period during which emergency action could be taken by a President.

As the debate went on, Senator Stennis and Senator William Spong of Virginia, who was managing the bill for the Foreign Relations Committee in conjunction with Senator Javits and me, recognized that the bill might pick up support if clarifying amendments were offered by the sponsors. Senator Javits, however, took the position that any perfecting changes should only be offered after a test vote had been taken on any amendment offered by the bill's opponents. Stennis, an old hand at parliamentary give and take, replied that this would be a tactical mistake. If any perfecting amendments had validity, they should be offered at the outset by the bill's sponsors, so as to demonstrate good faith and allay doubts that those who favored the proposal were frozen in their position. Stennis prevailed, and on April 5, 1972, the sponsors offered a three-amendment package to the War Powers Act. The first of the three amendments dealt with the President's emergency authority to act in any situation on the high seas involving a direct and imminent threat to the lives of

American citizens. Initially, the sponsors of S. 2956 had argued that the bill's emergency provisions covered attacks or the imminent threat of attacks on American citizens anywhere outside the boundaries of the United States. They agreed, however, that this perfecting amendment would clarify that point beyond any doubt.

The second amendment dealt with the assertion that the thirty-day authorization period was an unconstitutional limit on the President's emergency authority to repel enemy attacks. To clarify this, the sponsors proposed to give the President authority to certify that "unavoidable military necessity respecting the safety of armed forces of the United States engaged pursuant to Section 3 (1) or 3 (2) of this Act requires the continued use of armed forces in the course of bringing about a prompt disengagement of such hostilities." In order to exclude the possibility that the President could interpret the word "disengagement" to include a slow withdrawal such as had occurred in Vietnam, I offered the sponsors' definition of that word:

> I draw a sharp distinction between the word "withdrawal" and the word "disengagement," and this amendment was drafted with that distinction in mind. I see the action of withdrawal as being indefinite and ongoing. The word disengagement on the other hand, [has] two dimensions. It encompasses the full meaning of the word withdrawal but also includes the strong implication of finality. . . . By using the word disengagement in this amendment, we seek to require a complete divorce from prior policy considerations. The President would be obligated not only to withdraw U.S. forces from the hostile situation but also

would be required to cease his pursuit of the objectives for which he initially involved them in hostilities.

The third perfecting amendment related to the charge that the NATO unified command would be adversely affected by the War Powers Act. The following new language was offered:

> Nothing in Section 3 (4) of this Act shall be construed to require any further specific statutory authorization to permit members of the Armed Forces of the United States to participate jointly with members of the Armed Forces of one or more foreign countries in the headquarters operations of high level military commands which were established prior to the date of enactment of this Act and pursuant to the United Nations Charter or any treaty ratified by the United States prior to such date.

As Stennis had predicted, the introduction of these amendments seemed to open the way to final passage of the War Powers Act. While they did not altogether mollify Senators Goldwater, Dominick, and McGee, the amendment did erase some of the major criticisms made in debate. They also solidified Senator Cooper's support, and on April 5 the amendments were approved by a 59–0 vote. With that, the center seemed to go out of efforts to alter the specific provisions of S. 2956. Henceforth, the opposition would have to make a straightforward challenge of the bill's constitutionality and indeed, from the start they had argued that Congress had no authority to intrude upon that no-man's-land separating the constitutional warmaking responsibilities of the executive and legislative branches. It was their opinion that the

Founding Fathers had purposefully left the Constitution vague, so that the President might cut the cloth to fit whatever shape the future might take.

This was the thrust of the attack by Goldwater, Dominick, and McGee, who were joined by two ranking members of the Judiciary Committee—Sam Ervin, Democrat from North Carolina, and Roman Hruska, Republican from Nebraska. Ervin and Hruska argued procedure. They noted that the standing rules of the Senate assigned the responsibility for considering "constitutional amendments" to the Judiciary Committee. Since in their view the War Powers Act was really intended to amend the Constitution, they proposed that it should be referred to their committee. To the bill's supporters, Ervin and Hruska were attempting to strangle the initiative by stretching jurisdiction of the Judiciary Committee to cover a proposal which was not intended to amend but to fulfill the Constitution. The Senate was not being asked to vote on a procedural question of committee jurisdiction, but on the substantive issue of the act's validity. On April 11, 1972, the Ervin-Hruska amendment was decisively defeated, 26 to 60.

This test vote proved a portent. Amendment upon amendment was submitted in the next two days to weaken the bill or to destroy it. Each vote showed overwhelming support for the War Powers Act and seemed to weaken the resolve of the now dwindling opposition. An amendment by Republican Senator Glenn Beall of Maryland to create a commission to study the matter went down, 23–56. An amendment by Senator Dominick to substitute the language of the weak Zablocki bill was defeated 22 to 56. Support for S. 2956 was now running quite deep, and the administration was having trouble keeping its forces in line.

April 12, 1972, was what is referred to in the United States Senate as a long legislative day. The final vote came shortly before 9:00 P.M. on an amendment by Senator McGee, who proposed a national commission on United States foreign policy, which would examine the questions of our commitments and the exercise of war powers by the executive and legislative branches. At the root of the amendment was McGee's belief that S. 2956 was wrong. Senator Spong spoke for the sponsors. To accept McGee's change, he said, would "represent an uncertain trumpet to . . . [the Senate's] finished work on this legislation." He commended McGee for his initiative but added that he felt the concept of a national commission should be submitted as separate legislation and not as an addendum to the war powers bill. The Senate agreed; the amendment was defeated by a vote of 19 to 57.

As that long and tiring day drew to a close, it was apparent to all that only a national catastrophe could keep the Senate from passing the War Powers Act. Still, a small group of senators were discussing one final amendment by Senator Dominick to be introduced the following day. Dominick, by now convinced that S. 2956 would pass, stated that he was only seeking to give more power to the President under the emergency provisions of Section 3. At issue were Subsections (1) and (2) of Section 3. Under Subsection (1), the President had been given specific authority to retaliate in the case of an attack upon the United States. This authority was granted in consideration of a nuclear strategy that depended upon retaliation or a "second-strike" capability for defense of the nation. Subsection (2), which permitted the President to repel an attack on our armed forces stationed abroad, had excluded this right of retaliation. Now, however, some of the bill's sponsors were considering accepting Dominick's revision.

On the morning of April 13, Senator Javits, Stennis, Spong, and I met in Stennis' office to discuss the Dominick challenge. We agreed that it would not be necessary to give ground. But might not the amendment be right? Might not the authority to retaliate be necessary for the defense of our armed forces when attacked? I argued that acceptance of the Dominick amendment would seriously damage the bill and give the President wide latitude to retaliate without restraint. I pointed out that the bill did not prohibit American forces from defending themselves when attacked, by whatever means necessary. The Gulf of Tonkin incident was a case in point. Under S. 2956, a President could, I argued, authorize an attack on the home port of attacking North Vietnamese vessels, if he felt that our forces were in immediate peril. The bill would not, however, allow any retaliation that could not be fully justified as an act of self-defense. After long discussion, my colleagues agreed and we left for the floor of the Senate to complete our work.

The Dominick Amendment went down by a 19 to 59 count and the way was cleared for a vote on final passage. The only significant changes in the War Powers Act that had been adopted were the three perfecting amendments proposed by the sponsors and added at the outset of the debate. The final vote came at two in the afternoon on April 13, and the margin was 68–16 in favor of passage. Several Republican senators, who had supported referral motions and other crippling amendments under administration pressure, reversed themselves and voted aye. The bill had been blessed with bipartisan support from the start. Full discussion had served to deepen the Senate's understanding of the central issue—the responsibility of Congress to decide when and whether the nation should go to war. The intent was not to undermine the institution of the presidency nor assert any legislative omnipotence. The Senate was mindful, as it was put by Alexander M. Bickel, in the January 22, 1972, issue of *The New Republic*, that "there is no assurance of wisdom in Congress, and no such assurance in the presidency, on domestic problems or foreign. The only assurance there is lies in process, in the duty to explain, justify and persuade, to define the national interest by evoking it, and thus to act by consent. Congress will sometimes fail to give its consent to wisdom and hold out for foolishness. At such times, the President, who is differently constituted, has enormous leverage as a persuader, and great power as a brake. Singly, either the President or Congress can fall into bad errors, of commission or omission. So they can together, too, but that is somewhat less likely, and in any event, together they are all we've got. In emergencies requiring instant action, or for purposes of command decision, the President alone is all we've got, as the war-powers bill fully recognizes. But that is true only in emergencies."

9

Using the Power of the Purse

Nineteen seventy-two was a presidential election year, and Congress recessed during the months of July and August when the two major political parties met to select their candidates. The Democratic and Republican platforms reflected significant differences in their respective approaches to the role of government in modern America. Of special interest to me was the treatment of the war powers issue. The Democratic party, the party of such strong Presidents as Roosevelt, Truman, Kennedy, and Johnson, included the following resolution in its foreign policy platform: "Return to Congress, and to the people, a meaningful role in decisions on peace and war. . . ." The Republican party, the party of self-identified strict constructionist President Richard M. Nixon, made no reference to the issue. Other events of course preoccupied me in the summer of 1972, but the subtle shift of my party from espousal of the creative and dynamic executive to the relative safety of collective decision-making did not, in all the confusion, pass me by.

The "victory" won in the Senate the previous April was short-lived. After considerable delay, the "third House of Congress," the House-Senate conference committee, met in October 1972 and adjourned after one meeting, having failed to resolve major differences between the two houses. The failure was not unexpected. The two bills had little common ground. The careful delineation of the President's emergency authority and the automatic cutoff provision in the Senate bill were in sharp contrast to the simple reporting requirement in the Zablocki bill. With little more than a week remaining in the Ninety-second Congress when the conferees met, there was never any real chance that the gap between the House and Senate bills could be bridged.

One of the greatest struggles between the executive and legislative branches was underway, but the American people had yet to grasp its practical political significance. President Nixon's lopsided victory in November over Senator George McGovern seemed to demonstrate that the national government was still very much a presidential one, and although coming events would shatter the myth of the Nixon mandate, 1972 was the President's year.

On October 26, National Security Adviser Henry A. Kissinger, proclaimed that peace in Indochina was "at hand." Democratic presidential candidate McGovern noted that there were "at last reports that seem to have some substance that a cease-fire and perhaps an end to the war in Vietnam is approaching." A *New York Times* editorialist wrote:

> Henry A. Kissinger's firm assurance that "peace is at hand" in Vietnam and his confirmation of the agree-

ment announced by the North Vietnamese should go far to relieve doubts about the Administration's determination to end the United States' involvement in Indochina.

Some hard-core skeptics, wary of the timing of the announcement (the presidential election was but a few days away) were not so sure. "After so long a wait, and so many false flashes of light at the end of so many tunnels, there is a temptation to doubt everything until an agreement is signed," said a *Washington Post* editorial.

Throughout November and into December we waited. Then, on December 18, Dr. Kissinger announced with shocking suddenness that negotiations had been temporarily broken off. The bombing of North Vietnam resumed, with exceptional fury. The skeptics had been wise.

Popular outrage and indignation were matched by weariness and regret. In Congress, the antiwar movement came alive again. The administration was charged with having used the negotiations to insure its reelection. Senator Mansfield sensed a "volcanic upheaval against the war building up in the electorate. . . . The people's hopes were raised and they were led to believe peace was within reach. But now we are back in the same old tunnel and the lights have been dimmed again."

There was no immediate White House acknowledgment of a change in policy when the bombing was resumed without warning on December 18. The fact itself was acknowledged a few days later by a Pentagon spokesman, but no explanation was given, and no effort was made to reconcile the bombing and

Henry Kissinger's December 18 statement that talks had been only temporarily disrupted and would resume after the first of the year.

When the full extent of the bombing became known, the public was stunned. With the exception of a brief respite on Christmas Day, air strikes on Hanoi were relentless: despite Pentagon denials, we were carpet bombing the capital of North Vietnam, only indifferently discriminating between military and civilian targets. Foreign observers reported that hospitals, residential neighborhoods, and the foreign embassy community in Hanoi were hit. As the outcry over the air strikes rose to a crescendo, just five days before the opening of the Ninety-third Congress, on January 3, 1973—the bombing was stopped—as quickly and as mysteriously as it had begun. Perhaps the administration hoped to dampen the growing antiwar feeling before it could be translated into congressional action. If so, it succeeded, but the bombing left an indelible imprint on the public conscience. It would be easier henceforth to win sympathy for a legislative check on the President's power to do as he wished militarily.

Addressing the Democratic conference at the opening of the Ninety-third Congress Senator Mansfield said that the recent presidential election "tells us something of what the people of the nation expect . . . The people have not chosen to be governed by one branch of government alone. They have not asked for government by a single party. Rather, they have called for a reinforcement of the Constitution's checks and balances." * He urged a strong bipartisan move to end the war. "We cannot dismiss our respon-

* Despite the overwhelming victory of the President, the Democratic majority in the Senate increased by two, 57–43.

sibility by deference to the President's. It remains for the Congress to seek to bring about complete disinvolvement."

The next day, January 4, the Democratic conference voted overwhelmingly to "work to cut off all funds for U.S. combat operations in Indochina subject only to the release of our prisoners and the safe withdrawal of our troops." The resolution had been anticipated by the administration, but the size of the vote (twelve senators dissented) had not been. The message was clear: the people wanted peace now.

When Henry Kissinger returned to Paris, the real talks—the private ones—resumed, but a week would go by before news reports (most based on well-placed leaks) would suggest progress. When the President announced on January 23, "that we today have concluded an agreement to end the war and bring peace with honor," the reaction was more one of relief than elation. All emotions had been played out; "peace with honor" seemed anticlimactic. Very few thought that phrase meant victory.

The cease-fire agreement that finally emerged was acclaimed as a triumph for the negotiating skills of the American team headed by Dr. Kissinger. It was at once detailed (the cease-fire enforcement mechanism) and ambiguous (in its treatment of the political differences that were the root causes of the war). When Dr. Kissinger met with the press on January 24, his earlier "peace is at hand" statement seemed a faint and unimportant memory.

At about that time, Senator Javits, Senator Stennis, and I began all over again. Along with sixty cosponsors, we presented to the Senate the same War Powers Act (S. 440) that had passed overwhelmingly the previous April. But now there seemed to be keener interest in the subject, an interest enhanced by the recent real-life experience of unchecked presidential power.

Those who had long opposed the war and whose indignation was recharged by the Christmas bombing, were impatient, driven by their determination to prevent future Vietnams. We had purposely divorced our legislative effort from the Indochina situation, however, by stating that our bill would not apply to hostilities in which the United States was involved on the date of enactment. We had to do this to retain the support of Senator Stennis, but it later proved a source of confusion.

The polarization that had so long frozen congressional debate on the war seemed magically to disappear in January. To attack the President's power during an ongoing war had been intolerable to many, but with a peace agreement signed, the willingness to reassert congressional power was on the rise. This changed attitude was most clearly visible in the House, where prior attempts to pass war powers legislation had been discouraged as "dovish" moves to undercut the President.

Senate sponsors had also to take account of hard feelings that had been expressed by House members a year earlier over the handling of the Zablocki bill by the Senate Foreign Relations Committee. An olive branch was appropriate. So, in a Senate speech on January 29 I referred to a new bill introduced by Congressmen Zablocki and Dante Fascell and asked that we "begin an earnest and hopefully constructive dialogue to resolve differences of approach and to create legislation that will help us to regain the proper constitutional prerogatives of Congress." Congressman Fascell telephoned the next day to suggest that our staffs get together. Congressman Zablocki's staff asked my legislative assistant if I would like to testify before Mr. Zablocki's Foreign Affairs Subcommittee, which was considering war powers legislation.

Heavy pressure for some move had built up in the House since the December bombing. Many new members had been elected on a "stronger Congress" platform. A multitude of new war powers bills had been introduced in the House, and it was the job of the House Foreign Affairs Committee to deal with them. The first indication of cooperation from "the other side" was most welcome.*

Almost as soon as Dr. Kissinger completed his detailed explanation of the Paris Agreement, speculation arose as to its significance to the executive-legislative tug-of-war. According to the agreement, our forces would have to be totally withdrawn from Vietnam within sixty days of the January 27 signing date. But what about the possible reinvolvement of our forces after March 28? Would the President request authority from Congress if he felt such action was required? The question went to the heart of the controversy. It was an awkward political question, because Senator Stennis, who had insisted that Vietnam be left outside the bill's scope, was a key figure. When a *Washington Post* reporter asked for an interpretation of Section 9 (the applicability section) in the context of the agreement, it seemed to me time to bring this matter to a head. On the day of my "olive branch" speech, I walked over to Senator Stennis

---

* Instead of routinely reporting out the House bill with no comment, the Foreign Relations Committee waited until the end of the session and reported the bill to the Senate floor with a negative recommendation. Many House members considered this an unnecessary affront.

who was sitting near me and privately asked his view. He agreed with my interpretation: when the cease-fire was fully consummated, on March 28, any reintroduction of U.S. forces would have to have the approval of Congress, if by that date the war powers bill was law. However, Cambodia and Laos were different, he said. They would not technically come under the provisions of our bill until cease-fire agreements were signed in those two countries and our involvement terminated. I didn't share that view, but felt that those two countries could be handled separately.

In my judgment, Stennis' position on Vietnam in this context was extremely important. I didn't realize then, how important our discussion was. Two days later Senator Stennis was taken to Walter Reed Hospital in critical condition, shot by thieves as he arrived at his home that evening. One of the most powerful men in Washington, the chairman of the Armed Services Committee and a man whose decision to join the war powers effort had been pivotal, was out of action.

The shooting dominated the Washington scene for weeks but it did not keep Congress from discussing Indochina. I telephoned Senator Javits and proposed a joint statement on the applicability of the War Powers Act to the situation we would face on March 28, the day the U.S. withdrawal was to have been completed. I told him of my discussion with Senator Stennis and he immediately recognized its significance.

In presenting our interpretation of the act on February 20, Senator Javits and I tried to reflect as accurately as possible the position Senator Stennis had taken in private conversation two weeks before. We said that it was our understanding "that the cease-fire agreement will not be fully consummated until March 28, 1973, 60 days from the date of the signing. If on that date all other provisions of the cease-fire agreement are upheld by the signatory nations, American participation in hostilities within North and South Vietnam will terminate. At such time and in accordance with Section 9, the provisions of S. 440 would, on the date of enactment, apply in full to any reintroduction of forces to North and South Vietnam.

Senators Church and Case had previously (January 26) introduced legislation to cut off all funds for the U.S. military in Indochina after March 28, 1973. Though strongly supporting their initiative, I had some reservations about its timing, one day prior to the signing of the Paris Agreement. Congress and the people were for the first time in nine years seeing light at the end of the tunnel and were reluctant to think about the possibility that we could be led back into the darkness. I later announced support for the Church-Case bill, but only after the March 28 cease-fire deadline.

Euphoria is the word to describe how the American people felt during March. Large groups of POWs were flown at weekly intervals to Clark Air Force Base in the Philippines and subsequently home. Each planeload provided the TV-viewing public with a heart-rending glimpse of those unfortunate men, some of whom had spent as long as eight years in North Vietnamese prisons. But this was no VE-Day or VJ-Day celebration. The Vietnam War was ending as it began, gradually.

But could we be sure it was ending? In a February appearance before the House Foreign Affairs Committee, Secretary of State William Rogers had been evasive when asked if he could see any circumstances which would cause the President to recommit American troops to Vietnam. "I'm really not going to speculate about the future," he said. When Congressman John Culver of Iowa sought clarification, Rogers sounded insulted: "I don't think this is the time to criticize the President for actions which have been so successful." The remark was a portent of things to come.

At the urging of Washington, the Lon Nol government in Cambodia had offered in early February to abide by a de facto cease-fire. When this offer was turned down by the Khmer Rouge, the United States employed massive bombing to force compliance. Yet there had been little reason for the administration to expect the insurgents to accept a cease-fire. The Khmer Rouge were quite strong. As the focal point for a number of previously dissident Cambodian factions, they found themselves in February 1973, in control of approximately 80 percent of the territory of Cambodia. United with their former antagonist Prince Norodom Sihanouk in an uneasy but effective political alliance, they could claim absolute command of the countryside. And while they were outnumbered two to one by Lon Nol's forces, they held strategic routes to the capital city of Phnom Penh. Heavy U.S. bombing notwithstanding, they must have sensed ultimate victory.

Article 20 of the Paris Agreement dealt with Cambodia and Laos. It was an ambiguous provision and for obvious reasons—the parties to the conflict in those two countries were not signatories to the agreement. Article 20 had no deadlines and no enforcement or arbitration devices, as did the sections of the agreement affecting North and South Vietnam. In general terms, Article 20 required the withdrawal of all foreign armed forces from Laos and Cambodia. Section (c) also said:

> The internal affairs of Cambodia and Laos shall be settled by the people of each of these countries without foreign interference.

Did this mean what it seemed to say? The administration alluded to an informal agreement reached in Paris, under which the United States and North Vietnam would use their powerful patronage to encourage a cease-fire and negotiations. But when it appeared in February and March that the North Vietnamese would not do that, the administration sought to force the hand of the North Vietnamese by a devastating bombing blitz. Thus, an estimated thirty thousand North Vietnamese forces assisting the Khmer Rouge were the means for introducing the people of Cambodia to the B-52 bomber.*

The bombing ravaged the Cambodian countryside for two straight months. On March 29, 1973, the President went on national television to state, "We have ended the longest and most difficult war in our history in a way that maintains the trust of our allies and the respect of our adversaries." Closing his speech with a poignant story about the courage one POW derived from an abiding faith in God and country, he said, "If we meet the great challenges of peace that lie ahead with this kind of faith, then one day it will

---

* U.S. government estimates of North Vietnamese troop strength in Cambodia was approximately thirty thousand, with two to five thousand actually engaged in combat with Khmer Rouge forces. The remainder of the North Vietnamese force remained in the sanctuary area on the South Vietnam border, and most were support forces.

be written, this was America's finest hour." Yet at that moment, we were waging a different kind of war over Cambodia and Laos—one that had no Hamburger Hill, no Pleiku; a war that could easily be overlooked by the American people, for its toll in American lives was slight. (We did lose eight men, however, when an EC-47 went down in Laos in February prior to a cease-fire agreement in that country.)

The first hint of how the administration might justify continuing combat operations in Indochina after March 28 came at a luncheon meeting held by Deputy Assistant Secretary of State William Sullivan, Dr. Kissinger's deputy during the Paris negotiations. When asked what authority the President would have to continue hostilities, Sullivan said, "For now I'd just say the justification is the reelection of the President."

Five days after the President's speech declaring the end of the Vietnam War, I criticized the continued bombing of Cambodia in a Senate speech, calling it unconstitutional and immoral. I also pointed out that although the agreement signed in Paris was not a legal document under domestic law, its implicit imperative was the complete withdrawal of American forces from Indochina. The last semblance of any unilateral presidential authority to engage in hostilities in that area had vanished with those forces. I noted, "The President has, perhaps coincidentally, fulfilled the 'policy of the United States,' as expressed by Congress, to withdraw all U.S. military forces from Indochina 'at a date certain,' subject to the release of American prisoners. This policy was established in the Mansfield Amendment to the Selective Service Act of 1971 and the Defense Procurement Authorization Bill of 1971. The Mansfield Provision was not legally binding on the President. But whether the fulfillment of its objectives in the Paris Agreement was coincidental or not, the President cannot in light of that provision, now assume that he has been delegated the authority of Congress to reinvolve the United States in Indochina."

I cited the Javits amendment to the Supplemental Foreign Assistance Act of 1970, which Congress had approved:

> Military and economic assistance provided by the U.S. to Cambodia and authorized or appropriated . . . shall not be construed as a commitment by the U.S. to Cambodia for its defense.

In light of this legislative record, the President was, in my mind, acting illegally in carrying on the bombing:

> The Paris Agreement does not contradict the law, but the actions the Administration has taken in the name of that Agreement do constitute such a contradiction. If the lawful position on Indochina as expressed by Congress requires changing, it will have to be changed by Congress acting with the President—not by the President acting alone.
> The real sum of these alleged justifications is that the President has no constitutional authority to do what he is doing.

The administration was being pressed on several fronts. The afternoon I spoke, Secretary of Defense Elliot Richardson, who had come to Capitol Hill to testify on the defense procurement bill, was questioned about the President's actions. Richardson replied that the bombing was necessary "to clean up a messy corner of the war." Mr. Nixon, he said, could use the authority he had been previously granted; he therefore required no additional authority. That was interesting. Whereas the White House had earlier claimed that its authority derived from a responsibility to protect American personnel in Indochina, it was now saying that the same authority justified intervention "to clean up a messy corner of the war," though there were no longer any American servicemen in Indochina to protect.

In the weeks that followed, the administration offered no serious legal rationale for what it was doing. Then on April 30, 1973, a full month after the total withdrawal of our forces, the State Department came forth with a memorandum entitled "Presidential Authority to Continue U S Air Combat Operations in Cambodia," in which the President's role as commander in chief was linked to his responsibility to enforce Article 20 of the Paris Agreement:

> . . . Unilateral cessation of our US air combat activity in Cambodia without the removal of North Vietnamese forces from that country would undermine the central achievement of the January agreement as surely as would have the failure by the US to insist on the inclusion in the agreement of Article 20 requiring North Vietnamese withdrawal from Laos and Cambodia. The President's powers under Article II of the Constitution are adequate to prevent such a self-defeating result.

The transition from what may be good policy (though many in Congress thought it was not) to what is good law is not so casually made. If unilateral enforcement of the Paris Agreement was acceptable under prevailing political standards, the methods employed in pursuit of that aim did not meet the criterion of constitutionality. In the absence of congressional authorization, our combat operations in Indochina were illegal. In insisting on his inherent power to conduct these operations over Cambodia and Laos, the President was preventing Congress from exercising its powers under Article I, Section 8 of the Constitution. The State Department simply ignored this, as usual. Instead, the department constructed a case based on a self-defined, self-assumed obligation on the part of the commander in chief to uphold an executive agreement—an agreement which did not have the force of law.

Legality aside, the President quite plainly *could* order the military to bomb. And the Congress could not stop him, could not reclaim its own dominion over war, since the courts had refused to rule on a "political question." Never had the delicate fabric of the Constitution been stretched so thin. The "twilight zone" described by Justice Jackson as separating the war powers of the executive and legislative branches was occupied by the President.

The Indochina bombing was costing money, however, and the administration could not forever defer replenishing the Pentagon's budget. Its request for additional funding came in the second supplemental appropriations bill of 1973, a normally routine measure used to supplement agency budgets when unforeseen circumstances cause a shortfall at the end of the fiscal year. Devaluation of the dollar had put a squeeze on all U.S. foreign operations. A number of agencies desperately required supplemental funding, none more so than the Department of Defense, the agency with the most extensive operations abroad and the one charged with the bombing of Cambodia.*

There was no direct request for war-related funds. Instead, in a March 21 letter from Director of the Office of Management and Budget Roy Ash, the White House asked for an increase of 500 million dollars which it could transfer *within* the Pentagon budget. The amount was more than sufficient to sustain the bombing. In testimony before the House Defense Appropriation Subcommittee on April 12, Acting Defense Department Comptroller Don R. Brazier reluctantly conceded, that "US air operations in support of Cambodia would be included in the $500 million." In fact the entire sum would have been available under the broad charter of the transfer authority.

Administration strategy became obvious the first week of May: congressional approval of the transfer authority would be cited as legal sanction for U.S. combat in Cambodia. The State Department's legal memorandum had been highly criticized in Congress and in the media, and the administration badly needed to legitimize what it was doing. One of the points made by the State Department in its April 30 memorandum now took on additional impact:

> The Congress has cooperated with the President in establishing the policy of firmness coupled with an openess to negotiation which has succeeded in bringing about the Agreement of January 27 and which can succeed in securing its implementation. *This cooperation has been shown through consultations and through the authorization and appropriation process."* (Emphasis added.)

* Estimates by the Cornell University Center for International Studies indicate we were spending $4,800,000 daily for air operations over Cambodia.

As a new member of the Appropriations Committee, I listened attentively to Secretary Richardson on
May 7 as he explained that the President could go on
waging war in Cambodia, without congressional approval of the additional transfer authority:

> It must be emphasized, however, that the denial of the
> requested authority will not impact on U.S. air opera-
> tions in Cambodia. . . .

The next day Richardson was quoted in the *Washington Post* as saying, ". . . If an amendment were
offered to specifically restrict the use of any of those
[supplemental] funds for air support in Cambodia
and it was defeated . . . we would be justified in
regarding that vote as a vote to at least acquiesce in
that activity." So whatever we did, short of an absolute cutoff of funds, the President could do as he
liked. In cross-examining Secretary Richardson, I ex-
plored the administration's paradoxical legal position:

> SENATOR EAGLETON. Does the administration cite
> any authority other than article 20 of the Paris agree-
> ment as being a legal justification for the bombing in
> Cambodia?
> SECRETARY RICHARDSON. I would not argue and
> have not argued that article 20 in some sense confers
> authority specifically on the President. I am arguing
> that the authority he has now is the same authority he
> had as of the day the agreement was signed, and the
> day before that, and the month before that, and the
> year before that. Nothing happened then that dimin-
> ished it.
> SENATOR EAGLETON. Then is your argument or ra-
> tionale meant to infer that article 20 confers no new
> authority on the President?

SECRETARY RICHARDSON. That is right. It does give us an added reason for continuing to support the Cambodian Government because the continued presence of North Vietnamese forces in Cambodia is not only threatening the survival of the cease-fire agreement in South Vietnam but is in specific violation of article 20 itself.

SENATOR EAGLETON. If there is some other authority—and since article 20 confers no new authority there must be some justification from the administration's point of view for the bombing—what is that legal authority over and above article 20?

SECRETARY RICHARDSON. The point is that—

SENATOR EAGLETON. Legal authority.

SECRETARY RICHARDSON (continuing). As I said, I am not prepared to undertake a recital of distinctions of the President's legal authority as of January 27.

SENATOR EAGLETON. The Gulf of Tonkin Resolution which has been repealed—or is it SEATO?

SECRETARY RICHARDSON. No.

SENATOR EAGLETON. Is it the Commander in Chief power?

SECRETARY RICHARDSON. Are you asking me whether on January 26 the President had legal authority to bomb in Cambodia?

SENATOR EAGLETON. You said article 20 conferred no additional authority on the President. You stated that he had the same authority on the 27th that he had on the 26th.

SECRETARY RICHARDSON. Yes. Why do I need to point to any new authority? If he had authority on January 26, the cease-fire agreement did not take it away.

SENATOR EAGLETON. I am trying to find out what that authority was on the 26th as you view it today. It is not SEATO. It is not Tonkin. Is it the Commander in Chief clause?

SECRETARY RICHARDSON. I am not prepared to answer that question because I had not supposed as of January 26th anybody challenged the President's authority to support the Cambodian Government by air.

SENATOR EAGLETON. The Commander in Chief authority is the only one I imagine, hinged on the premise of the safety of American troops and POW's which was accomplished on the 30th. I assume whatever authority he had vanished on the 30th when the POW's were returned and the troops were withdrawn. Your justification here is solely based on article 20. It mentions no other precedent or authority for the bombing in Cambodia other than article 20.*

SECRETARY RICHARDSON. Your question is that unless I can find some new basis of authority the President does not have it. My answer is that I don't need to do that, because the President's authority as of the day before the cease-fire agreement was not terminated by the cease-fire agreement.

On May 10, the House took up the second supplemental appropriation bill of 1973, and Appropriations Committee members Joseph Addabbo of New York, Clarence Long of Maryland, and Robert Giaimo of Connecticut led the onslaught on their chairman, George Mahon of Texas. The first important vote came on an Addabbo amendment to knock out the 500 million dollars in additional transfer authority funds for the Pentagon. The amendment passed, 219 to 188. Congressman Long introduced an amendment prohibiting the use of any funds in the bill to pay for combat activities in Cambodia. This also passed, 224 to 172. But that did not stop the President. True, the denial of funds in the supplemental bill would be a

---

* The reference is to March 30, the date when the last POW was recovered from the Viet Cong in South Vietnam.

strain, but Secretary Richardson had already said that the operation would not suffer; other forces and operations around the world would be cut back. That's the way the game would be played, unless and until the Congress got its message across in far tougher terms.

That need was foremost on my mind as the Senate Appropriations Committee met on May 15 to consider the supplemental bill, now returned from the House. My concern was shared by some rather unlikely colleagues, such as Senator Norris Cotton, Republican from New Hampshire, and Senator Milton Young of North Dakota, the ranking Republican on the committee. The amendment to the supplemental bill by Senator Long barred money for combat operations in Cambodia. Long's amendment was broadened by Senator Brooke of Massachusetts to include Laos, where the United States had briefly resumed bombing when the cease-fire in that country broke down. But the Long and Brooke language applied only to funds in the supplemental bill. I wrote on my pad, "or heretofore appropriated under any other act . . ." These seven words transformed the House language into an absolute cutoff of funds for combat activity in Cambodia and Laos, the two remaining theaters of the Indochina War. I asked Senator Fritz Hollings of South Carolina, who sat next to me, to check my handwritten addition. When he agreed it was "foolproof," I asked to be recognized. I moved to amend the House bill, and to my surprise the committee accepted my motion, 24–0. At the time, it seemed a rather routine decision, but in retrospect the unanimous vote by the traditionally conservative Appropriations Committee was momentous and took the administration completely by surprise. The White

House could only stall the floor vote, while marshaling support for its position. The first indication of White House action came when Senator Roman Hruska reversed his committee position and requested additional time as permitted by committee rules to draft a minority opinion to the committee report. So the bill was temporarily held up.

By mid-May the cease-fire violations in Vietnam were becoming a conspicuous embarrassment to the administration. The breakdown of the truce was bringing harsh words from hawks who thought the administration had given up too much in Paris. And the Cambodian War became the target for a fast-growing antiwar contingent. To head off this double-barreled onslaught, Dr. Kissinger was sent back to Paris to shore up the original agreement with Hanoi's negotiator Le Duc Tho. That had had an inhibiting effect on criticism in the past, and administration spokesmen resurrected the old appeal: "Congress shouldn't rock the boat during sensitive negotiations."

In a major address on May 19, Mr. Nixon introduced a new element into the political equation when he charged Hanoi with failing to make a full accounting of Americans missing in action. It was Armed Forces Day. The President spoke alongside the aircraft carrier *Independence* in Norfolk, Virginia:

> It would be a crime against the memory of those Americans who made the ultimate sacrifice for peace in Indochina, and a serious blow to this country's ability to lead constructively elsewhere in the world, for us to stand by and permit the settlement reached in Paris to be systematically destroyed.

The supplemental appropriation bill and the Eagleton amendment reached the floor of the Senate on May 29. Administration forces chose to attack my amendment indirectly on parliamentary grounds. The parliamentary question raised was whether I was attempting to legislate on an appropriations act, which is prohibited under Rule XVI of the Standing Rules of the Senate. My staff had checked this question with the Senate parliamentarian and found that a point of order raised in the context of Rule XVI *would* be sustained, and my amendment disallowed. But there was a rarely used parliamentary tactic for getting around such a ruling. According to Senate precedent, I could raise a "question of germaneness." If I could win that vote, it would obviate a ruling from the chair and override Rule XVI.

As expected, Senator Hruska raised a point of order on my amendment, and in accordance with a previous unanimous consent agreement, we set aside one hour to debate his point. I was struck then as before at the civility parliamentary procedures force on the most emotional debates. Senator John Tower of Texas warned his colleagues that an "evil precedent" would be established if the Senate voted to override Rule XVI. Senator Robert Griffin of Michigan said that I was trying to "scuttle the rules of the Senate in order to somehow show the White House who is boss." Minority Leader Hugh Scott of Pennsylvania said that the precedent of overriding the Senate rules "will rise to plague us."

I reserved argument on germaneness, concentrating instead on the substantive merits of the amendment and the administration's paradoxical legal position:

A careful examination of the Administration's position will demonstrate how Congress has been stripped of its options. On the one hand, then Secretary of Defense Richardson stated that the defeat of any amendment which would specifically restrict the use of funds for air support over Cambodia would be considered "as a vote to at least acquiesce in that activity." If, on the other hand, a restriction is approved limiting only funds within this bill, again according to Richardson, the Administration will continue the air operations anyway, using money appropriated for other defense purposes. We are left, therefore, with no room for compromise.

I urged my colleagues to take this opportunity to regain a decision-making role for Congress:

. . . In the past three years, we have made our case to the American people loud and clear. We complained that the President was fighting a war without our consent . . . that the President did not inform us . . . that the President has not asked for our authorization . . . that the President has usurped our war powers. Over and over we have exposed the constitutional argument to our constituents. Now, according to a recent Gallup Poll, a full 76% of the American people believe that continued involvement in Indochina should be a matter for Congress to decide.

We can no longer hide behind the Presidency. We can no longer put off our responsibilities to await the latest word from Paris. And we can no longer rationalize that our individual vote—even though only one of 535—is unimportant. Now, because we have made the American people aware of the role Congress must play within our governmental system, we will be held individually and collectively accountable for the action we take.

At the end of the time allotted for the point-of-order motion, I raised the issue of germaneness and addressed the charge that I was trying to shatter the rules of the Senate. I argued that the House of Representatives had already proposed legislation on the instant appropriations bill. And I quoted from the Senate's guide to parliamentary procedure:

> If the House of Representatives opens the door by incorporating legislation in a general appropriations bill, the Senate has an inherent right to amend such proposed legislation, and to perfect that language, notwithstanding its rules.

A large number of senators had come to the floor in expectation of the pending vote. Several expressed surprise that there was precedent for overriding Rule XVI. Many would have undoubtedly voted with me anyway, but not so many if it had been necessary to set aside Senate rules and procedures. On this crucial vote, the Senate by 55–21 declared my amendment germane to the House-passed language.

As expected, the opposition wouldn't permit an immediate vote on the amendment. It needed time to develop a new strategy, which was forthcoming. Two days later, I was confronted with two opposition amendments which the proponents said would simply modify the language of the amendment. In reality, they would have transformed my motion into an authorization for limited war.

The first amendment, proposed by Senator Robert Taft of Ohio, would have added the following "except" clause:

> Except as to combat activities by air operations against the forces of the Democratic Republic of Vietnam

which by their presence in Laos and Cambodia are in violation of Article 20 of the Agreement of ending the war and restoring peace in Vietnam, dated January 27, 1973.

Taft argued that my amendment would give our adversaries an incentive to break the terms of Article 20, if it did not grant the President authority to bomb areas where North Vietnamese troops were located. I countered by attempting to demonstrate the military impracticality of his amendment and then addressed the legal significance of the Taft clause:

> What the Taft amendment would do, if agreed to, would be to make Article 20 of the Agreement in Paris the codified law of the United States. It would, perhaps unwittingly, be another Gulf of Tonkin Resolution in so far as the Cambodian War is concerned. It would authorize indefinite American participation in air raids over Cambodia for the purpose of seeking out North Vietnamese troops wherever our military commanders think they might be. Under this open-ended authority, the President would then have the unilateral authority to bomb ad infinitum.

When Taft was defeated 63–17, I turned to a potentially more serious challenge from Senator Dole. Dole wanted to delay any cutoff of funds until the President certified that the government of North Vietnam had made a full accounting of all Americans missing in action. His proposal had considerable emotional appeal. He charged the North Vietnamese government with purposely withholding information about our MIAs and said that continued military pressure was necessary if we were ever to get a full accounting.

I shared Senator Dole's concern, but despite the President's speech of May 19 and Senator Dole's comments, the administration had made no formal protest on this matter to the International Control Commission (ICCS) established by the Paris Agreement. A four-party joint team had been set up to implement the portions of the cease-fire agreement relating to the missing in action. Any member of this team could issue a formal complaint with the ICCS if another member was not cooperating. I had received an advance copy of testimony to be delivered that afternoon by Frank A. Sieverts, special assistant to the deputy secretary of state for POWs and MIAs. Sieverts would say that the North Vietnamese were cooperating (at their own pace) and that the joint team had already made two visits to Hanoi to inspect the graves of Americans killed in action. I said it would be a tragic irony to authorize war in another part of Indochina, while we were engaged in recovering MIAs from North Vietnam. Since the January 27 cease-fire, two Americans had been lost in Cambodian operations and were listed as missing in action. "Yet the Senator from Kansas wants this body to give legal sanction to combat activity which is adding Americans to the missing." Dole's amendment was rejected 56–25, and the Senate then immediately adopted the cutoff amendment in its original language by an overwhelming margin of 63–19.

Why was the Congress now ready to flex its muscles after nine long years? Perhaps the single most important reason was the widespread fear that the United States might not yet be out of the woods. The situation in Cambodia was frighteningly similar to the one in South Vietnam during the Diem years. Each administration move to support the beleaguered

Lon Nol government reminded Americans of that earlier experience. In addition, the euphoria that accompanied the release of our POWs had been somewhat tempered by a deep concern that those unfortunate men had been held longer than necessary, hostages to the negotiating sessions in Paris. We were losing pilots in Cambodia, and there was anxiety that a captured pilot would become a new bargaining chip. The President might renew the offensive, so as to force the release of the newly captured Americans.

Another factor was the President's declining popularity. A series of shocking disclosures of White House complicity in an attempted break-in at Democratic National Headquarters had seriously weakened Mr. Nixon's credibility. The "Watergate affair" had lowered his personal popularity from a high of 68 percent just after the January 27 cease-fire announcement, to 45 percent at the beginning of May. Now, as we appeared poised to fight still another war in Indochina, the people were seriously searching for ways to circumscribe presidential power.

10

Compromised Out

By the spring of 1973, we were dealing with a President who seemed to feel that the only legitimate restraint which could bind him was the political acceptability of his initiatives. We in the Congress tried to counter this philosophy of expediency with an expediency of our own. We attacked the effects of the abuses of power, but we were reluctant to address the cause—the erosion of congressional authority. Nowhere was this reluctance better exemplified than in legislative maneuvers to end the Cambodian War. Kissinger returned to the United States after his first round of talks with Le Duc Tho on May 23, with no new agreement or understanding. With the Senate's adoption of the Eagleton amendment on May 31, the President was being backed into a corner. The administration needed much more than hints of progress to come, it needed a tangible accomplishment. Kissinger was sent to Paris again on June 5 to resume the talks.

The amendment went to the House-Senate conference with strong support from many House members. Congressman Mahon chaired a hawkish contingent of House conferees, and there was little disposition among them to accept the amendment. They determined to stall in order to allow the administration more time to negotiate a Cambodian cease-fire. There was little the Senate side could do about it; we had been assured by Mahon that he would report the amendment out in disagreement, a procedure which would permit a House vote on the merits of the amendment.

Kissinger returned to Washington on June 9, amid reports that South Vietnamese President Thieu would refuse to accept a proposed joint communique designed to implement the cease-fire agreement. During earlier negotiations, Kissinger's job had been complicated greatly by the need to bargain not only with North Vietnam, but with President Thieu as well.

The awkward three-way negotiation was another reminder of the futility of our endeavors in Southeast Asia. Successive Saigon regimes never had great popular appeal, and now again Saigon was being obstructionist. Kissinger publicly said he would not allow South Vietnam to disrupt the negotiations. His frustration was apparent when he was asked on June 9 to explain the delay in light of previously optimistic remarks by other members of the U.S. delegation: "American officials have sometimes been mistaken in their estimates of the length of time required to bring the Vietnamese parties to a common realization of the significance of certain words." It was reported soon thereafter that the South Vietnamese were told in no uncertain terms that they would "lessen their objections or face the likelihood that U.S. reconstruction aid would be cut back." When Kissinger flew back to Paris on the eleventh some sort of agreement appeared to be imminent.

The announcement that finally came on June 13 was a disappointment. It did not end American combat activity. Kissinger acknowledged that nothing in the communique "commits the United States to cease bombing" Cambodia. The failure was readily apparent. The *Washington Post* said in an editorial:

> The Kissinger shuttle has had the appearance of an unseemly overreaching American effort to manipulate those domestic events in Vietnam which we had thought the January Agreement had left to the Vietnamese. . . . Why should the signatures be worth more in June than in January? Is this to become a regular semi-annual affair?

Congress wasn't buying the subterfuge. On June 14, one day after the communique was signed, the Senate passed a State Department authorization bill which contained the Case-Church amendment. Sentiment ran so strongly in favor of a fund cutoff that the President's supporters didn't even try to strike the end-the-war provision. The bill passed by a 67–15 vote and numbered among its supporters Senator Hugh Scott, Republican minority leader. Scott explained his vote succinctly: "We have had it!"

Kissinger's globe-trotting was not over. This time he was off to China, ostensibly to continue the dialogue opened the previous spring during President Nixon's visit. Upon his return on June 24, Kissinger let it be known that he had solicited Chinese help to end the fighting in Cambodia: "We are pursuing the subject of negotiations with Hanoi. We are prepared to listen seriously to the views of others who also have an interest in bringing the war to a conclusion."

The message was familiar: sensitive negotiations were underway, give us time.

This was the atmosphere on June 25 when the House considered the Eagleton amendment—the first absolute cutoff of funds for ongoing combat activity in our history. After three months of delay, a supplemental appropriations bill initially described by the administration as "urgent" had finally been reported out of conference. The House conferees dis agreed that it should be adopted but they were now giving the full House a chance to vote on the issue. Congressman Mahon, who had opposed the original Long amendment restricting only the use of money appropriated in the bill itself, now defended that amendment as the "House version." He argued that it was not the intention of the House in voting for the Long amendment to be as "all-inclusive" as the Eagleton amendment. He moved that the House support its conferees' position on the amendment, whereupon Congressman Giaimo offered a "preferential motion" that the House "recede from its disagreement." "The issue here," said Mahon, "is shall we recede and capitulate to the Senate. Shall the House capitulate and take what is interpreted by many as an indefensible act at a time when negotiations are underway and when the chances appear good that the war in Southeast Asia will indeed be brought to an honorable and reasonable and satisfactory conclusion."

Congressman Giaimo spent little time going over old ground. He simply wanted it made clear that the House's intent in passing the Long amendment was to stop the bombing. This was not, however, the administration's interpretation of that amendment; thus the need for the Eagleton amendment. Congressman

Gerald Ford, then minority leader, made the final plea for the pro-administration forces: "We just have to, in my humble judgment, be firm and strong in the waning minutes of the most important ball game that we have played in this body in a long time." But that line, effective so often during the Vietnam years, would fail this day. The House agreed to the Senate language, 235–172.

Congressman Mahon then moved to amend the Eagleton amendment, so that it could not be effective until September 1, 1973. It was a skillful maneuver, attractive to those who felt uneasy about a complete cutoff. He wished to give the President "two additional months in which to try to work out a solution in Cambodia which will not leave Cambodia a major threat to the ceasefire in Vietnam." But to give the President that time, Congress had to sanction a heretofore unauthorized war, a point that was made by Congressman Ogden Reid: "I think the Constitution is clear . . . that Congress should decide and Congress should be the branch to declare war. Frankly, I think the American people have made a judgment that this war should be ended, so I hope the House will vote down the Mahon amendment and assume the responsibility to end the war and the bombing now." The House did assume that responsibility, but by the narrowest of margins, a tie vote of 204 to 204. Congressman Gunn McKay, who had voted with Mahon, withdrew his vote and voted "present."

So for the first time, Congress sent to the President a bill mandating an absolute cutoff of funds for ongoing combat, and it did so during the last week of the fiscal year, when the President's options were narrowing. He needed money to run the government.

Because the budgetary cycle is somewhat behind the fiscal year changeover, Congress normally must pass a "continuing resolution" to enable the agencies of government to operate for a prescribed period into the new fiscal year. What would happen if such a resolution were not enacted? Chairman Mahon answered that question when he opened debate on the continuing resolution June 26: ". . . the US Government would fall on its face the US Government would come to a screeching, grinding unacceptable halt at midnight on June 30. . . ." Despite that ominous prospect the House challenged the President by again adopting the language of my amendment, 240–172.

The next morning the President vetoed the supplemental appropriations bill and charged that

> . . . the 'Cambodia rider' to this bill would cripple or destroy the chances for an effective negotiated settlement in Cambodia and the withdrawal of all North Vietnamese troops, as required by Article 20 of the January 27 Vietnam Agreement.

Urging Congress to rush the supplemental bill through before the end of the fiscal year—minus the Cambodia rider—the President cited the impact of the other provisions of the bill on the operations of the government: "By June 28, nine government agencies will have exhausted their authority to pay the salaries and expenses of their employees. The disruptions that would be caused by a break in the continuity of government are serious and must be prevented. For example, it will be impossible to meet the payroll of the employees at the Social Security Administration which will threaten to disrupt the flow of benefits to 25 million persons." In sum, re-

sponsibility for disrupting government was Congress'
not the President's. Not one word in the message
dealt with the President's legal authority for conducting combat activities in Cambodia.

I had entertained some small hope that the President would sign the bill and end the bombing. Senator John Tower, a long-time supporter of the President's Indochina policy, had said that he was
"inclined to think the President will not veto the
bill." White House Deputy Press Secretary Gerald
Warren said that Nixon would consult with congressional leaders before deciding whether to sign or
veto the legislation. The President did not consult.

A few minutes after hearing of the veto I called
Senator Mansfield to discuss what could be done. He
suggested that we pass the amendment again as soon
as possible. After checking the legislative calendar,
he called me back and asked if I could get my amendment ready in short order to be brought up on the
debt ceiling bill. I said yes.

Our government operates at a temporary debt ceiling to allow for a controllable amount of deficit
spending. Periodically Congress approves this temporary ceiling, which in 1973 was 65 billion dollars
over the permanent ceiling of 400 billion established
in 1971. If the government were to stop spending at
the higher ceiling, it would have to immediately stop
any new outlays in order to pay its debts. If the President were to veto such a measure, the effect would
be disastrous.

By the summer of 1973, confidence in the dollar
had dropped to a new low. The shock of moving into
a new fiscal year without the debt ceiling authorization would have brought economic chaos. It was a
prospect I was sure Richard Nixon could not relish.

Senator Russell Long, chairman of the Finance Committee and one of the few Democrats who opposed my amendment, wasn't happy that I was about to complicate a normally routine bill. Nevertheless, he promised to defend the will of the Senate in conference:

> . . . Let me say that I recognize that this amendment, if agreed to, means a very serious confrontation between the legislative and executive branches. . . . I will not vote for the amendment. If it is agreed to, I will do my duty and will support it in conference and will see to it that the House has an opportunity to vote on it.

When the Eagleton amendment to the debt ceiling bill passed by a 67–29 vote, the attitude of the Senate toward the President's veto was unmistakable.

About the same time on June 27, the House was attempting to override the President's veto of the supplemental bill. The override effort failed by thirty-five votes, or a turnaround of only eighteen. That vote was the strongest antiwar showing to date in the House. Combined with the Senate vote on the debt ceiling bill, it was an impressive show of strength. The White House must have sensed the growing sentiment for an immediate cessation of the bombing. Former secretary of defense and now Presidential Counselor Melvin Laird was assigned the task of salvaging the President's policy. That was another first—the executive branch was actively bargaining with Congress over its right to continue a war that had never been authorized.

The bargaining was done between Laird on behalf of the White House and the members of the Senate Foreign Relations Committee, the original catalyst of congressional anti-war sentiment. If a compromise were to be effected, the White House knew that it would have to gain the consent of this committee.

On the afternoon of June 29 when I arrived at the Senate chamber for the debate on the Continuing Resolution, the Foreign Relations Committee was meeting in closed session to vote on a compromise worked out between Laird and certain members of the committee. By then a consensus had been reached. The constitutional crisis, which would take place on July 1 if the vital money bills were not enacted into law, must be avoided. The final language would not be approved until later that afternoon by the administration, but committee members described their offer: if the President would accept the Church-Case provisions with the cutoff date set for August 15, then Congress would not press the Eagleton amendment. The war would have to end on that date, but the price Congress would pay for that was authorization of a 45-day Cambodian War. Only two members of the committee, Muskie and Mansfield, were unwilling to pay that price and voted against the compromise.

There was considerable delay before the compromise amendment was brought to the floor. The minority leader, Senator Scott, was awaiting final White House approval for what was to become known as the "Fulbright amendment." Senator Hartke started the debate a little early when, hearing of the compromise agreement, he decried what he called the capitulation of Congress. "I am unwilling to have Congress commit suicide," he exclaimed. "The proposal adopted by the Foreign Relations Committee is a declaration of war, and I am willing to stay here during all this holiday . . . while we decide whether we have the courage to stop the bombing and killing once and for all."

Senator Hartke's reference to a "holiday" was not an idle one. When Congress disposed of the end-the-year appropriations bills it would adjourn for the July 4 vacation. If the President were to veto a war cutoff provision, he would also surely call Congress back into session the next week. And he would keep it in session until one side or the other backed down

At about six in the evening word was received that the President had approved the compromise language and the debate began. The large number of senators in the chamber attested to its importance. Senator Fulbright read the amendment he would offer as a substitute to the Eagleton amendment:

> Notwithstanding any other provision of law, on or after August 15, 1973, no funds herein, heretofore or hereafter appropriated may be obligated or expended to finance the involvement of United States military forces in hostilities in or over or from off the shores of North Vietnam, South Vietnam, Laos, or Cambodia.

"The present amendment is, in essence, the result of an accommodation of the views of the committee and the White House following a meeting this morning," he said. Then Senator Fulbright performed a legal sleight of hand: "The acceptance of an August 15 cut-off date should in no way be interpreted as recognition by the committee of the President's authority to engage US forces in hostilities until that date." Senator Scott then concurred in Fulbright's interpretation.

Fulbright, Scott, and others had naturally emphasized that the amendment would "preclude" combat activity once and for all after August 15. But I was worried about what it would include until that date. I began my portion of the debate asking Senator Fulbright that question:

MR. EAGLETON. In the light of the legislative history, meaning the statement of former Secretary of Defense Richardson that we will continue the bombing unless the funds are cut off, will we with the adoption of this resolution permit the bombing of Cambodia for the next 45 days?

MR. FULBRIGHT. Until August 15.

MR. EAGLETON. Would it permit the bombing of Laos?

MR. FULBRIGHT. It would not prevent it.

MR. EAGLETON. Would it permit the bombing of North and South Vietnam until August 15?

MR. FULBRIGHT. I do not think it is legal or constitutional. But whether it is right to do it or not, he has done it. He has the power to do it because under our system there is not any easy way to stop him.

I do not want my statement to be taken to mean that I approve of it or think that it is constitutional or legal for him to do it. He can do it. He has done it. Do I make myself clear?

MR. EAGLETON. In a way yes, and in a way no. If we adopt this resolution, the President will continue to bomb Cambodia. That means quite simply that we will sanction it, does it not?

MR. FULBRIGHT. We do not sanction it. It does not mean that we approve of the bombing. This is the best way to stop it. I have never approved of it. And I do not wish my answer to indicate that I approve of the bombing, because I do not.

MR. EAGLETON. But the President will exercise a power to bomb in Indochina within the next 45 days, is that correct? A power that will now be sanctioned by our action?

MR. FULBRIGHT. The President has the power to do a lot of things of which I do not approve.

MR. EAGLETON. He will exercise that power, and whether he exercises that power wisely, we know that within the next 45 days he will exercise a right to bomb Cambodia—a right given him by the Congress of the United States.

Senator Mansfield put the full force of his office in direct opposition to the compromise amendment: ". . . What we will be considering shortly is not an accommodation with the Chief Executive of this country, but a capitulation and an abdication of the constitutional powers of the Senate." He was followed by Senators Hatfield, Kennedy, and Bayh who likewise opposed the compromise.

Senator Church then defended the compromise he helped fashion as a member of the Foreign Relations Committee. He said that acceptance of the compromise would not mean that the Senate "is somehow giving its blessing to an unconstitutional war . . ." Calling that a "novel" position, he said "this is not the first time that a deadline has been placed in an amendment to end the war."

That argument was central to the position of the Foreign Relations Committee. But in my opinion it failed to consider that the only unilateral constitutional authority the President could claim after the repeal of the Gulf of Tonkin Resolution was the power to protect forces on the battlefield.

I conceded that previous resolutions had established deadlines, but pointed out that those time limitations were based upon vastly different conditions. "That was a time when there were half a million American combat troops on the ground in South

Vietnam," I said. "And the alleged excuse for the troops being there at all, after the Gulf of Tonkin Resolution was repealed, was that the President was protecting those troops—and that he needed time to draw down the troops—and that he wanted, as some have expressed it, to avoid a Dunkirk-type situation."

American forces were no longer in Southeast Asia; they had been removed under the terms of the Paris Agreement. And along with them went the last semblance of presidential authority to conduct war. There was no escaping the effect of the compromise amendment; it would provide the President with the legal authority he had previously lacked to continue the bombing.

The practical threat of a presidential veto had more force with many senators than did any constitutional question. Many felt that a governmental crisis had to be avoided at all costs, even if it meant that war was to be declared. This view was expressed by Senator John Pastore: "I say this is going to be an act of contrition for everyone in this Chamber who votes for this compromise, but, short of voting for the compromise, what is the alternative? The alternative is that the President will go on indefinitely unless we tie up the mechanism of government, and each alternative is really bad."

But I never believed that the President would bring the government to its knees simply to continue bombing Cambodia. The White House was talking tough and the veto of the supplemental bill two days before gave some credence to those threats. But up to then the President had never had to make a hard choice. Already weakened by the Watergate disclosures, he would have been extremely hard-pressed to risk fiscal chaos only to provide a temporary prop to the government of Lon Nol. He had sacrificed nothing by vetoing the supplemental bill, but a veto of the continuing resolution would have placed his administration in real danger.

I spoke to this political consideration in response to Senator Pastore:

> Mr. President, it is our duty to appropriate funds so that the Government can operate. And by passing vital appropriations bills prior to the end of the fiscal year we are performing that duty. But it is also our solemn duty to decide how, when and where our Nation goes to war. And by attaching a cut-off amendment to these bills, we perform our duty according to our own sense of it.
>
> But the President has a duty as well—a duty to carry out the laws as enacted by Congress. And he has a duty to assure that the Government of the United States continues to operate into the next fiscal year. If he chooses to reject the appropriations we provide him for that purpose, then he must accept the full responsibility for the consequences of that action.

The consequences of a shutdown of government were, of course, far-reaching. The President had spoken of Social Security checks, Senator Pastore of a shutdown of veterans' hospitals. But it seemed to me that the presidency, which commands so much political power in the age of modern communications, was at a distinct disadvantage in this particular confrontation. If the government stopped because he refused to sign the legislation necessary to make it run, his pursuit of the Cambodian policy would appear to be an obsession. I was confident that Richard Nixon understood the weakness of his position.

Later, as the evening of debate drew to a close,

Senator Fritz Hollings told how he sat with me in the Appropriations Committee two months earlier and helped create the Eagleton amendment. He told how he had refused to yield to Chairman Mahon in conference. "In fact," he said, "I kiddingly . . . said, let us get Jim Allen [a member of the Rules Committee with jurisdiction over the Senate restaurants] and put the Eagleton amendment on the Senate menu, on everything we possibly can get it on, to make clear that we do not want to slip sidewise into another Gulf of Tonkin."

But the President's offer of a compromise was too tempting. After more than a quarter century of denied and foresaken power, Congress was now bargaining with the President as an equal. Or at least it appeared that way. The vote to authorize war until August 15, was 58–31. The House would ratify the bill the following day. The crisis was over.

After twelve years of combat in Indochina, Congress finally ended our involvement by authorizing it for forty-five more days. Legally, the war should have ended in January 1971, when the Tonkin Resolution was repealed. But it would not end until the President ended it, on the President's terms.

The debate of June 29 was the best I had participated in in five years in the Senate. The missing element was accountability. Few Americans would have held Congress responsible if the forty-five-day war had led to renewed involvement. Only the President would have been blamed. That is not the intent of the Constitution, but that is what our system of warmaking had become. And when, on August 15, U.S. military operations in Indochina officially ended, I wondered whether the sacrifice of Congress' war powers was worth it. Perhaps this time it was. But how would America next go to war? And how would that war be terminated?

11

Legislative Language and the Realities of War

Senator Fulbright had assured the Senate in good faith on June 29 that his committee agreed to the compromise over ending the Indochina War on the assumption that "the interval between now and August 15, will not be the occasion for an escalation of U.S. bombing in Cambodia. . . ." One week later the Pentagon confirmed reports that bombing sorties over Cambodia had been increased by 50 percent since June 30. No, this was not an escalation, the administration insisted; we had simply taken advantage of the weather. Obviously, the White House was going all out to force a cease-fire before August 15.

Senator Walter Mondale of Minnesota called the bombing "indefensible" and accused the administration of violating the compromise agreement. But if an agreement had been violated, it was only an informal one between Richard Nixon and the individual members of the Foreign Relations Committee. The law now allowed the President to conduct military operations in Cambodia. Command decisions were his to make for forty-five days. Pentagon spokesman William Beecher made this clear in a press briefing on July 2, when asked whether the increased sorties violated the spirit of the compromise:

> The Administration is anxious to conclude a cease-fire in Cambodia. . . . It will try to use its authority to conclude that cease-fire.

Had the spirit of the compromise been violated? The clamorous discussion of that question in the early days of July had a familiar ring. In the summer of 1967, the Foreign Relations Committee had held hearings during which it was asserted that the Gulf of Tonkin Resolution was not meant to sanction all-out war. But Undersecretary of State Nicholas Katzenbach had firmly rejected that view in an angry exchange with the senators:

> Didn't that resolution authorize the President to use the armed forces of the United States in whatever way was necessary? Didn't it? What could a declaration of war have done that would have given the President more authority and a clearer voice of the Congress of the United States than that did?

Nine years after the Tonkin resolution, Congress still seemed unmoved by the potential danger of blank-check delegations of its war powers. In the *New York Times* of July 19, I wrote: "It is now more apparent than ever that Congress will not exercise its war powers unless legislation is enacted clearly reaffirming that we must bear the responsibility for authorizing war. . . . Considering the President's most recent claim of power—a broader claim than has ever been made before—and Congress' willingness to sanctify that claim by a false compromise, I feel we must enact the most carefully and tightly drawn bill possible."

The war powers bill passed by the Senate the previous April was a strong one, but in order to get it through we had had to yield ground to the executive. For example, Senator Stennis had felt that the effectiveness of our nuclear strategy depended not only on our deterrent capability but also on our being able to threaten a first strike. He wanted legislation that would not even hint at prohibiting preemptive attacks. So his original bill, which in most other respects resembled my own, gave the President authority "to prevent or defend against an imminent nuclear attack on the United States by the forces of any foreign government. . . ." In an October 8, 1971, letter to Senator Stennis, to which I agreed in advance, Senator Javits pointed out the dangers of the Stennis clause:

> From a political and diplomatic viewpoint, I foresee drawbacks in separately authorizing the President to wage, in effect, preventive nuclear war. It seems to me that this might be misinterpreted as signalling a very important shift in U.S. strategic doctrine, away from the "second strike" posture we have always maintained, toward a "first strike" or "launch on warning" posture.

We then offered new language which we felt would preserve the integrity of America's deterrent strategy, while allowing a degree of ambiguity acceptable to Senator Stennis. We stated that in addition to the President's power to repel attacks, he would have the right to "forestall" such attacks if they were "direct and imminent." We held that this "forestall clause" was consistent with our nuclear strategy but proposed that the legislative history make plain that a first-strike attack was not being sanctioned by Congress. The power to forestall, we said, was a logical extension of the President's right to repel attacks. The legal basis for this position could be found in an opinion by Justice Story in *Martin* v. *Mott:* "The power to provide for repelling invasions includes the power to provide against the attempt and danger of invasion as the necessary and proper means to effectuate the object."

Even with the "direct and imminent" proviso, I was troubled that we had allowed the President too much leeway. The "forestall clause" would give him considerable discretion, especially considering that the United States had over two thousand military installations overseas. I was more fearful than ever about a President getting us into war by attacking preemptively on the basis of intelligence estimates unavailable to Congress.

The Cambodian bombing policy of the President moved me in another direction as well. The previous year, Senator Stuart Symington, my senior colleague from Missouri, and his Subcommittee on United States Security Agreements and Commitments Abroad had exposed the "secret war" in Laos. Our government had, since the early sixties, used civilian employees of the Central Intelligence Agency in a combat role, organizing indigenous Laotian forces to engage in hostile action. Yet the war powers bill dealt only with the "Armed Forces of the United States"; it did not cover civilian combatants.

On July 2, William E. Colby testified before the Armed Services Committee with respect to his pend-

ing nomination as director of the Central Intelligence
Agency. Colby had been in charge of the controversial Phoenix program * while stationed in Vietnam,
and he knew well the covert side of our intervention.
When asked to explain the CIA operation in Laos,
Colby said, "It was important that the U.S. not be officially involved in that war." Colby was referring to
foreign governments when he said we should not be
"officially involved," but future CIA directors might
find themselves trying to circumvent Congress in
much the same manner.

Word came soon after the July 4 recess that the war
powers bill would be brought to the floor. I therefore
sought through staff discussions to determine if Senator Stennis would object to a move to strike the forestall clause from the bill. Not surprisingly, he *would*
object.

According to his staff, Senator Stennis did not,
however, feel as strongly about another proposed
amendment: striking Section 9, the section which
would have excluded ongoing hostilities from the
provisions of the bill. Now that Congress had approved the August 15 cutoff date, this provision was
no longer pertinent. Our original agreement was to
insert language which would exclude the Vietnam
War. But the end of the war had already been mandated by legislation, so I felt no compunction about
dropping the provision.

The second week in July, I sent a list of four proposed amendments to Senators Javits and Stennis for

---

* "Phoenix" was the code-name for a CIA-sponsored counterinsurgency plan designed to expose Viet Cong sympathizers in the provinces. One of the methods allegedly employed by our Vietnamese allies
to eliminate suspects was assassination.

their comment. Two were in the "housekeeping" category; one to correct a simple typographical error and a second to straighten out a poorly drafted section. The others were the amendment to cover civilian combatants under the provisions of the bill (I called this "the CIA amendment"), and one to strike Section 9 and make the bill effective on the date of its enactment. Senator Javits suggested that we meet the following week to discuss the changes.

On the day I was to meet with Javits, I had a telephone call from Senator Stennis. "I won't oppose the other amendments, Tom, but I wish you would drop the CIA matter." He, too, was concerned about the agency exceeding its authority and promised to look into that question as chairman of the special committee overseeing the CIA. I told him that I felt strongly about the amendment, that I appreciated his special interest and would welcome his effort to revise the CIA charter, but that the war powers bill had to cover the possibility of civilian combatants, whether employees of the CIA or some other government agency. He said he had no choice but to oppose me. I understood that and regretted that we could not agree.

Later that day, I assured Senator Javits that the housekeeping amendments would be handled routinely. He concurred and we went on to the amendment to strike Section 9. He reminded me that the agreement to exclude the Indochina War was instrumental in getting Senator Stennis to support the bill. He agreed that the question was moot, but asked that I put off the amendment until the end of the debate on the bill.

I had entertained some hope that Senator Javits, who had spoken out in the past against the "secret war" in Laos, would support my CIA amendment. He would not, however, risk losing Senator Stennis' support. I told him, "If we don't cover civilian combatants in the bill, we will almost encourage Presidents to use them in lieu of uniformed personnel." I wanted both him and Senator Stennis to understand that this was a new element that had not been raised at the time of our original agreement or in subsequent talks. He said that he would have to oppose the amendment.

Knowing that both Javits and Stennis were against the CIA amendment did not exactly give me confidence in its ultimate success. They were not only effective advocates of war powers legislation, they represented the two committees most directly concerned—foreign relations and armed services. I would have dropped the matter had I not been so convinced of its necessity. Win or lose, it was important that the issue be aired on the Senate floor. Nonetheless, it was not comforting to be at odds with my two cohorts.

On July 18 the House passed H.J.Res. 542, the revised Zablocki war powers resolution, by a vote of 244–170. Ironically, the concept that had drawn the most criticism from the House Foreign Affairs Committee, the automatic cutoff provision, was now part of the House bill. The time period had been changed, from 30 to 120 days, but it was the same approach used in the Senate bill. The number of days would clearly be negotiable, since both bills allowed a cutoff by positive congressional action even before the specified period expired. We were approaching common ground.

But the House still insisted on what Congressman Zablocki called the "performance test" as a substitute for delineating the authority of the branches in taking the nation to war. The House bill contained no legal standard by which to judge any of the excessive claims of unilateral executive power. Congress would simply wait until *after* the President committed U.S. forces, and then decide whether or not he had acted properly. But such an approach would distort the intent of the Constitution. Difficult as the problem might be, Congress could not rightly avoid defining the President's unilateral emergency powers. Nor could we fail to insist that, in all other cases, Congress must authorize any commitment of American forces to war. The House bill sidestepped the authority question, and in so doing it neatly sidestepped the Constitution as well.

S.440, the Senate war powers bill, was also taken up by the Senate on July 18, although there was no plan to complete action on the bill that day. I again voiced concern over the implications of Congress' decision to authorize war in Indochina until August 15:

> The erosion of congressional war powers is manifested not only in expanded claims of Presidential power, but also in the lack of awareness Congress has for its own constitutional responsibilities. The recent decision to grant the President authority to bomb in Cambodia until August 15 demonstrated that, despite the rhetoric, some in Congress still believe that the President has the primary role in the decision to go to war.

As for the Javits-Stennis-Eagleton compromise bill:

> Certain aspects of the compromise bill before us today were somewhat troublesome for me, just as I am sure

Senators Javits and Stennis would have preferred their own approaches to war powers legislation. . . . One issue that was discussed at great length . . . was the matter of recognizing the President's power to "forestall" an attack on the United States or on American forces stationed abroad. . . . My original bill only recognized the Commander-in-Chief's power to repel sudden attacks. It did not specifically acknowledge his power to forestall such an attack.

Although I would not move to strike the forestall clause, I felt obliged to discuss the discretion it gave to the President. Senator Fulbright had already criticized this clause in his "Additional Views" to the committee report on the bill, but I considered his remedy more dangerous than the ailment itself. He would have replaced the section delineating the President's emergency powers with a general statement allowing the President "to respond to such action or situation [which] in his judgment constitutes a national emergency. . . ." Both Senator Fulbright and I were trying to limit executive discretion, but our legislative approaches were miles apart.

Debate on the bill began at 9:00 A.M. on July 20. My noncontroversial amendments were accepted without a vote by Senator Javits and Senator Muskie, who was managing the bill for the Foreign Relations Committee. The CIA amendment had substantial opposition.

"The bill before the Senate, S.440, is entitled 'The War Powers Act,'" I said. "But according to its preamble, S.440 does not cover all of the war-making alternatives available to the President." I urged my colleagues to "make the language of legislation match the realities of war," and pointed to the genesis of the Indochina involvement.

There was no Pearl Harbor to signal the beginning of the Vietnam war. There was no major attack such as the attack on Fort Sumter. There was no sinking of the *Maine*. There was only a gradually escalating involvement—an involvement which grew out of a political commitment and a mostly covert effort to fulfill that commitment.

We should have learned by now that wars do not always begin with the dispatch of troops. They begin with more subtle investments . . . of dollars and advisors and civilian personnel.

In the case of Laos, our involvement began with a large group of CIA advisors who organized indigenous Laotian forces to engage in hostilities in pursuit of policy objectives established by the executive branch of the U.S. Government.

Although the exact date remains classified, the CIA began to organize and advise Meo tribesmen in Laos sometime prior to 1961. This advisory role continued after the 1962 accords which ostensibly reaffirmed the neutrality of Laos and divided political control of that country among the warring factions. In testimony before the Symington Subcommittee on U.S. Security Agreements and Commitments Abroad, former Ambassador to Laos William Sullivan argued that our clandestine involvement in the Laotian hostilities was "to attempt to preserve the substance of the 1962 agreements."

It is not my intention today to question the merits of the policy Ambassador Sullivan was attempting to justify by his statement. I am simply advocating that the President present his justification to Congress, and that he request specific statutory authorization before he pursues a policy objective by means of force.

It was not, in my view, simply a matter of adding another clause to the legislation. If we were to exclude a particular method of making war, we risked encouraging a President to utilize that method to circumvent the statute. "If we fail to pass this amendment," I warned, "we may see an even more wide-ranging use of civilian combatants in lieu of uniformed personnel whose activities will be circumscribed by this bill. . . ."

Senators Javits and Muskie were reluctant but exceedingly formidable opponents. Senator Muskie agreed that Congress needed "greater control over the paramilitary activities of the CIA," but he called for a review of the CIA "in accordance with the normal legislative procedures of the Senate." Senator Javits saw my amendment as opening the bill to "substantive issues which are to be considered and decided in terms of the 'due process' we are establishing by this legislation." He said that the concept advanced by the bill was a "neutral methodology" that should not be subject to "substantive policy proscriptions on sensitive issues." Thus, he concluded that my amendment, however worthy, was "out of place." A letter from Senator Stennis was then read by Senator Muskie, in which Stennis reaffirmed strong support for the bill and then went directly to my amendment:

> The experience of the C.I.A. in Laos, as well as more recent disclosures of matters here at home have caused me to definitely conclude that the entire C.I.A. Act should be fully reviewed.
>
> Accordingly, I already have in mind plans for such a review of the C.I.A. Act by the Senate Armed Services Committee and have already started some staff work thereon. All proposed changes, additions or deletions can be fully developed and hearings held thereon at that time. I have already completed, but have not yet

introduced some amendments of my own. The proposal by the Senator from Missouri, Mr. Eagleton, to explicitly prohibit any action by the C.I.A. of the type we have had in Laos, or any other activity of that kind could and would be fully considered by the Committee at that time. I could support some major points in that particular amendment as a part of a bill on the subject, but fully oppose the amendment presented as a part of the War Powers Bill.

"This bill was not conceived in the abstract," I answered in rebuttal. "It was not conceived in the ethereal blue. It was conceived in blood—50,000 dead and the whole litany of what occurred in Southeast Asia. That is why we are debating this bill today—not because it is a prosaic idea, but because of our recent tragic experience."

By this time, Senator Fulbright had come to the floor to offer welcomed support. He had been trying for years to impose more stringent congressional control over the CIA. Two weeks earlier, his Foreign Relations Committee had taken the unprecedented action of rejecting the nomination of G. McMurtrie Godley to be assistant secretary of state for Far Eastern affairs, citing Godley's role in running the "secret war" when serving as ambassador to Laos. He described the CIA amendment as "an essential part of this overall legislation" and expressed regret that "every time an effort is made to assert the role of Congress in such matters, there are always reasons raised in connection with past practices as to why it should not be done."

Nevertheless, those "reasons" were to prevail again. The amendment was defeated 34–53. It was not a wasted effort, since Senator Stennis had promised to look into the CIA charter. So the chances for stricter congressional supervision of the clandestine activities of our government appeared brighter.

Senator Javits next agreed to strike Section 9 and the bill passed later that day 72–18 and was sent to conference to be reconciled with the House bill. I was sure it would be a long and drawn out process. The two Houses had agreed on the automatic cutoff concept, but there was no similarity whatsoever on the central question of prior authority.

Then on August 3 each congressman and senator received a copy of a cable sent to all military commanders by the secretary of defense. Entitled "Precluded and Permitted Defense Department Activities in Laos and Cambodia After August 14," it was a one-of-a-kind order to cease combat activity because of a congressional prohibition. The key paragraphs read:

> Effective at midnight on August 14 (Eastern Daylight Time) all combat activities of Defense Department forces are forbidden in, over or off the shores of Cambodia and Laos. This action is in keeping with Public Laws 93–50 and 93–52.
>
> Secretary of Defense James R. Schlesinger is issuing guidance to field commanders. Public Laws 93-50 and 93-52 prohibit any and all of the following activities: bombing, strafing, armed air reconnaissance, helicopter gunship operations, forward air control operations, artillery fire control or the employment of combat advisors with indigenous forces.

And yet the war wasn't over. On August 6 an American B-52 mistakenly bombed the village of Neak Luong, a key outpost of the Lon Nol government on the Mekong River. According to the American embassy in Phnom Penh 131 persons were killed and another 118 wounded as the center of the town was wiped out. Other towns had undoubtedly been hit the same way during the seven months of intensive bombing, but this one was held by our ally, and so the disaster was thoroughly reported by the American press.

The next day the friendly village of Tachor was hit by another misdirected American bomb strike. Eight persons were killed and sixteen wounded in the attack by a U.S. fighter bomber. Even the President's staunchest supporters now urged him to stop the bombing before more tragic mistakes were made. The *Chicago Tribune* stated in an August 10 editorial, "The innocent casualties caused by erroneous bombing in the last three days persuade us that Mr. Nixon would help himself and the country by ordering an immediate stop to bombing. . . ."

One week before the bombs fell on Neak Luong and Tachor, Justice William O. Douglas had ordered an immediate suspension of the bombing, comparing his controversial decision to staying the execution of a condemned man in a "capital case." He was acting on an appeal to stop the bombing by New York Congresswoman Elizabeth Holtzman, who on July 25 won a brief legal victory in the U.S. District Court of New York. The court order to suspend the bombing, issued by Judge Orrin Judd, was quickly stayed by the U.S. Court of Appeals for the Second Circuit before it went into effect. Congresswoman Holtzman appealed, first to Justice Thurgood Marshall, who ruled that he had no jurisdiction over the matter, and then to Justice Douglas, who reinstated the original order but was overruled on the same day by the full court. Whether Douglas was legally correct or not, his premise was prescient: "No one knows who the people to die might be, whether American military personnel or Cambodian peasants. The upshot is that we know that someone is about to die. . . ."

The Holtzman case caused the administration to plead that a cessation of bombing before August 15 would "cause irreparable harm to the United States." In a statement to the Court, Secretary of State William Rogers had said, "Any premature and unilateral cessation of needed air support would be seen by the government of Cambodia and many other governments as a breach of faith by the United States and would seriously undermine the credibility of the United States and impair the conduct of our foreign relations."

When the Supreme Court upheld the Court of Appeals' stay of Judge Judd's order, the legal question was indirectly resolved. Congress had given the President the statutory authority to bomb, if for no other reason than to maintain our "credibility." * The administration had met a limited test of legality, if not morality. To one woman of Neak Luong whose

* With the stay of the District Court's order in effect, the Court of Appeals passed on the merits of Representative Holtzman's claim on August 8, 1973. In overruling District Court Judge Orrin Judd, the Appeals Court held that the challenge to the legality of the bombing presented "a political and not a justiciable question." However, the court expressed the opinion that if the issue of legality *was* justiciable, passage of the Fulbright amendment would have constituted congressional approval. "Assuming arguendo that the military and diplomatic issues were manageable and that we were obliged to find some participation by Congress, we cannot see how this provision (the Fulbright amendment) does not support the proposition that the Congress has approved the Cambodian bombing," the court declared. On April 15, 1974, the Supreme Court announced that it would not consider the Appeals Court ruling, thus upholding it.

husband, a soldier, was killed by American bombs, the legality was unimportant. She could only ask, "Why did they bomb us?"

The *Baltimore Sun* said, "The whole thing, of course, is madness," and accused the administration of trying to set Congress up for blame if the policy (and the Lon Nol regime) were to collapse after August 15. But the public's perception of Congress' constitutional role was by now so distorted it did not matter that Congress had authorized a forty-five-day war. Except, of course, in the courtroom where the compromise was cited by administration lawyers to win their case to continue the bombing. When it all ended on August 15, few would agree with President Nixon's March 29 statement that our Indochina experience had been "America's finest hour."

The House-Senate conference committee * on war powers legislation was convened the last week of July. Senator Javits graciously asked that his staff assistant keep me informed of developments in the conference negotiations. The conferees met once before the long August recess, mainly to identify contentious issues and to get acquainted with each others' views. Although both sides were said to be courteous and accommodating, the dispute over prior authority sharply separated them, and it appeared that they were in for several months of debate.

Before the conference committee's next meeting, a position paper was prepared by Senator Javits and sent to each conferee. It was an excellent legal mem-

---

* The Senate conferees were Senators Fulbright, Mansfield, Symington, Muskie, Aiken, Case, and Javits. The House conferees were Representatives Zablocki, Morgan, Hays, Fraser, Mailliard, Fascell, Findley, Broomfield, and Frelinghuysen.

orandum and expressed serious reservations about the House bill. "The House text appears to be predicated on the assumption that the President will continue unilaterally to commit the Armed Forces to hostilities . . . without a declaration of war or prior specific authorization of the Congress." This assumption was challenged as a distortion of the Constitution. "Clarification of the underlying issue of authority is the essence of meaningful war powers legislation, for in recent years Presidents, in practice, have virtually monopolized the exercise of the war powers of the nation." I thoroughly agreed with Senator Javits' analysis.

But the House side was not going to submit peaceably. The House conferees prepared a rebuttal to the Senate position, which I received on September 18. The House seemed to accept literally the executive branch argument on the question of authority. In doing so, it rendered moot the "necessary and proper" clause, which enables Congress to legislate within the intent of the Constitution. "Even if the 'necessary and proper clause' is given its broadest construction, the House conferees said, "it is difficult to see it giving Congress the right to define the powers of the President. . . . [H. J. Res. 542] takes as granted that the Presidents will act on what they perceive to be their legitimate powers granted by the Constitution, or powers which they infer have been given them by past Congressional actions."

But the cardinal point was that we *had* been faced with a succession of Presidents who had boldly exercised their power to the exclusion of *any* congressional right to initiate war. The only leverage available to Congress under these circumstances was to use its power to legislate. The executive branch and the House conferees, however, believed that his power, found in the "necessary and proper" clause of the Constitution, should be forsaken.

On September 25 Senator Javits' assistant sent over a text of a counterproposal Senator Javits intended to make the following day "for the purpose of preserving the minimum essentials of the Senate position respecting the authority issue . . ." The key language defined the authority of the respective branches in the initiation of war:

The emergency powers of the President to introduce the United States Armed Forces into hostilities or situations likely to lead to hostilities being to (1) repel attacks upon the United States, its territories and possessions; (2) defend the United States Armed Forces abroad from attack; (3) rescue citizens and nationals of the United States; in any case in which the United States Armed Forces without a declaration of war by the Congress, or specific prior statutory authorization are introduced.

Following this statement were the procedures to be observed after entry into emergency hostile action. It was a minimally acceptable compromise from my standpoint, for although it was weak in circumscribing the President's power to rescue American citizens in danger abroad, it contained no reference to a "forestall" power, and that was potentially worth the trade-off. Most importantly, the congressional prerogative to authorize hostilities except in limited emergencies would have been preserved. If the House accepted the proposal, we would be well on the road to sending the bill to the President.

The conference committee staffs met frequently the following week, and the conferees convened again on October 3. By evening, they were close to agreement. When House Conference Chairman Zablocki left the meeting, he put his thumb and forefinger close together and said jubilantly, "We're only this far apart." The next morning the *Washington Post* reported that a "tentative agreement" had been reached, and that "the President would be authorized to take military action against foreign nations without the advance consent of Congress *in certain emergency situations,* but he would have to come back to Congress and obtain its express consent to continue the action beyond 60 days." (Emphasis added.) This was the general formula of the Senate bill, and while I was unsure what definition of the President's emergency powers had been used, I was pleased by what I read.

Senator Javits' staff assistant called that morning elated that the fundamental principles of the Senate bill had been preserved. Senator Javits had even insisted that the legislative language emphasize that the President could initiate action without prior congressional consent "only pursuant" to the emergency categories listed in the bill.

Then I obtained a draft copy of the bill. It contained a significant surprise. The authority provision was no longer under the "Reporting" section, it was now a part of a "Purpose and Policy" clause of the bill along with other general pronouncements of legislative intent. The authority language, found under Subsection 2(c) of the "Purpose and Policy" clause, seemed specific enough, authorizing only a limited range of presidential action. The addition of the word "only" seemed to make the clause even more restrictive. But why put the most important provision in a "Purpose and Policy" section, a section usually reserved for broad statements which are used for interpretive purposes in resolving questions relating to other sections? In this context it didn't seem possible that Subsection 2(c) was intended to be governing language, as was the case in the Senate bill. It didn't even track well with the provisions that followed. Something wasn't quite right and I asked my staff to thoroughly research the draft bill.

The conference report was by now printed, and it left little to the imagination. The key sentence describing the authority provision in Subsection 2(c) read as follows: "Subsequent sections of the joint resolution *are not dependent upon the language of this subsection* [referring to Subsection 2(c)], as was the case with a similar provision of the Senate bill." There was no longer any doubt about the conferees' intent. They were explicitly divorcing the interpretive definition of the President's emergency authority in the "Purpose and Policy" section from the legally binding portions of the bill. The authority language was not only not legally binding, but now even its value as a statement of policy was questionable.

What had finally been agreed to in conference did not simply water down the bill; it turned the Constitution on its head. By failing to define the President's powers in legally binding language, the bill provided a legal basis for the President's broad claims of inherent power to initiate war. Under the formula, Congress would not participate in the warmaking decision until *after* forces had been committed to battle. No specific congressional consent was required for ninety days (the bill called for congressional approval before sixty days but the President could simply certify that "unavoidable military necessity respecting the safety of US Armed Forces" required their continued use to extend his unilateral power for thirty more days). Congress could act by concurrent resolution to withdraw his authority at any time, but the fact remained that Congress could act only *after* the troops were deployed. Rather than tying the President's hands—as the White House surprisingly claimed—the bill would tie *Congress'* hands.

A disclaimer was added to the bill stating that it was not "intended to alter the constitutional authority of the Congress or of the President," but this was a meaningless statement since the judicial branch had historically refused to rule on challenges of authority by one branch against another when Congress had failed to pass a statutory definition of that authority. In addition, a provision was included to assure that a President could not cite the bill itself as statutory authority. But he had no need to cite the bill, since the only authority cited by recent Presidents was an "inherent" power derived from the commander-in-chief clause of the Constitution. Such a claim was improper and unconstitutional in my opinion, but no court would challenge it. It was a "political" question.

In brief, the conference bill was a dangerous piece of legislation which, if enacted, would effectively eliminate Congress' constitutional power to authorize war. It did contain the automatic cutoff provision, but Congress had been notoriously incapable of stopping a conflict once the flag had been committed. Once a battle is underway, the commander in chief controls the flow of vital information; the reins of power, political and military, are in his hands. Under these circumstances, it was unrealistic to expect a majority of Congress to oppose U.S. participation in an ongoing war, especially during the first weeks and months of the conflict when the President monopolizes public opinion. After all, it took nine years after the Gulf of Tonkin Resolution for Congress finally to stop the most unpopular war in our history. And that only after the troops had been withdrawn! If the conference bill passed, Congress would, for the first time, be surrendering its war powers by legislation.

12

Surrender

After three years of work, I now, sadly, had to oppose a war powers bill that would almost surely go to the President. It was not a decision that I relished.

Before speaking against the bill on October 10, I yielded time to Senator Barry Goldwater, who had been the staunchest opponent of the original Senate bill. Goldwater consistently held that Congress could not constitutionally restrict the President's actions, either before or after troops are committed to battle. But now he put forward an unexpected thought: "This conference report, Mr. President, I could probably actually vote for, because it gives the President even broader powers than the authors of the original bill thought they were correcting." I asked Goldwater to elaborate.

> MR. EAGLETON. Did I correctly hear the Senator say that in some respects he even considered voting for the measure, because this bill as presently drafted gives the President greater powers to wage one-man war than he had before?

MR. GOLDWATER. I would not vote for it under any circumstances.

MR. EAGLETON. I commend the Senator.

MR. GOLDWATER. But I do think that from the conference report, for example, it appears to me that the President is no longer prohibited from initiating original actions. He needs only to report during the first 60 days.

MR. EAGLETON. The Senator is precisely correct.

MR. GOLDWATER. This language puts into the law language that is not contained in the Constitution, but only assumed to be there because of the delegation of Commander-in-Chief powers to the President. If I were looking for a reason to change my mind, that would be it.

MR. EAGLETON. I agree with the Senator completely on that point.

I later told the senator that I hoped all one hundred of our colleagues had read the bill as carefully as he had.

And so we reached the beginning of the end. As debate opened, I conceded that the conferees must have had a hard time negotiating the authority issue, since both sides "marched down separate and distinct roads. . . ." Nonetheless, the final product was "a near-total abrogation of the Senate position on war powers." The authority provision contained under the "Purpose and Policy" section was "no more binding than a 'whereas' clause in a Kiwanis Club resolution." I then read what I considered the most telling sentence in the conference report, the sentence stating that subsequent sections of the bill were "not dependent upon" the authority provision. "If I were arguing a case to a jury of 12 good men," I said, "I would probably rest my case on that one sentence."

The conference bill was "worse than no bill at all,"
and I tried to explain why:

> It fails to address directly the question of just what au-
> thority the President has to engage our forces in
> hostilities without the approval of Congress. It is of
> questionable constitutionality in that it creates a
> 60-to-90-day period of Presidentially declared war, in
> derogation of the war powers conferred by the
> founders on Congress. And it creates a legal base for
> the continuing claims of virtually untrammeled Presi-
> dential authority to take the Nation to war without a
> prior congressional declaration.
>
> [The bill's] practical effect would be to enshrine, to
> make permanent by statute, the President's current
> misuse of power through a procedure which seeks
> only to limit that misuse rather than to prohibit it al-
> together.

Senator Javits disagreed with my interpretation
that Section 2(c), the authority section, was nonbind-
ing language and sought to disavow the perplexing
definition of that section in the conference report:
"There is nothing in the managers' report that makes
the legislative history exclusively or which binds the
Senate only to those confines. I am just as much a
manager . . . as the managers of the House." * If the
senator could successfully divorce himself from the
conference report he signed, then his contention that
the definition of authority in Section 2(c) was legally
binding might seem credible. He persisted with his
central point, that the entire bill had equal legal
force: "If this is a statute, every part means some-

---

* "Managers' report" and "conference report" were used in-
terchangeably during the debate, as were the words "managers" and
"conferees."

thing, whether it is written in Section 2(c) or in Section 3, as in the Senate bill."

The issues were joined. Was Section 2(c) legally binding? Was the Senate bound to the "confines" of the sentence in the conference report stating that subsequent sections of the bill were "not dependent" on Section 2(c)? Could Senator Javits disavow the conference report he signed? The answers to these questions would only come clear in debate:

MR. EAGLETON. . . . with respect to section 2(c), . . . the Senator realizes and has stated in his remarks that language relating to emergencies was in the operative section of the Senate bill, S. 440. Is that not correct?

MR. JAVITS. I do not agree with the Senator as to the definition of the "operating section." I think every section of this bill is operative, including the declaration.

THE PRESIDING OFFICER. The Senate will be in order.

MR. JAVITS. So I cannot accept the fact that the Senator chooses to make his own definition as to what is operative.

MR. EAGLETON. The Senator realizes, does he not, that it is an established legal doctrine? I have one "hornbook" * here—I could quote the Senator a hundred—that a preamble or a policy section is:

> To supply reasons and explanations and not to confer power or determine rights. Hence it cannot be given the effect of enlarging the scope or effect of a statute.

Is that not pretty standard, garden variety legislative law?

MR. JAVITS. But nonetheless this is a statute, and

---

* A "hornbook" is a law-school textbook which summarizes the study of case law.

every word in the statute, in my judgment, has equal effect, no matter what took place at the head of the column; in this case it is "purpose and policy."

MR. EAGLETON. Did not the conferees on the House side, the Zablocki side, fight very vigorously to keep it out of the operative sections and put it in the purpose and policy sections?

MR. JAVITS. "The operative sections" is strictly the Senator's definition. What they fought was making the touching-off point for the number of days the question of authority rather than the question of performance, and upon that, as I have stated before, we had to give ground, and we did.

MR. EAGLETON. I have one other question, and then I shall yield to the distinguished Senator from Mississippi, and then after that I shall have some concluding remarks of my own.

The Senator, in his presentation, said something to this effect—and I want to get it straight—that we are not to pay any attention to the managers' report; is that the gist of it?

MR. JAVITS. No.

MR. EAGLETON. The Senator signed the managers' report?

MR. JAVITS. I signed the report of the conferees. That does include the managers' report. We do not sign, as I understand it, the managers' report per se. The signatures appear at the end of the measure.

MR. EAGLETON. The signatures appear both at the end of the bill and at the end of the managers' report.

MR. JAVITS. That is right.

At this point, Senator Marlow Cook came over and whispered, "The Vice President has just resigned." The galleries were buzzing with the news and senators were coming to the Chamber seeking more information. Spiro T. Agnew, the thirty-ninth Vice President of the United States, had just pleaded *nolo contendere* to a charge of income tax evasion and had been given a suspended sentence of one year and a ten-thousand-dollar fine.

When order was restored, the debate continued with more discussion of the report and the conferees' responsibility for it. Senator Javits now argued that he was not trying to disavow the report, he was elaborating on it. But a subsequent judicial review would refer only to the bill and its conference report. Senator Javits' elaboration could not be accepted as the official congressional definition of the provisions.

Having exhausted that topic we went back to the bill itself. Despite the compromise with the House, was it still an effective control over presidential power? Senator Javits thought it was:

MR. JAVITS. . . . I say to the Senator from Missouri, as one of its original sponsors and one of the stalwarts with respect to the bill, let us not miss the forest for the trees. The fact is that never in the history of this country has an effort been made to restrain the war powers in the hands of the President. It may not suit my colleague 100 percent, but it will make history in this country such as has never been made before.

MR. EAGLETON. Mr. President, . . . we are not here to make history. We are here to make law. We are here to make important law, the most important law that can be made by man on this earth; namely, when to go to war—how, why, and when to go to war. . . . The fact is, we have a War Powers Act. It is what it says. That is important, not the title and not even the length of time that has gone into the making of the bill, as long as that has been. That is important, yes. But what is truly vital is how this Nation goes to war and what this bill says, not what the . . . intent of the Senator from New York was when he managed the bill on the floor of the Senate, but what this bill says now after it has come back from conference.

Yes, I helped to give birth to the Senate bill three years ago, but the child has been kidnapped. It is no longer the same child that went into the conference. It has come out a different baby—and a dangerous baby, Mr. President. Because this bill does not go one inch in terms of restricting the unilateral war-making of the President of the United States.

Try as he may, and able lawyer that he is, the Senator from New York cannot get around the language of the statute. He cannot get around the fact that the purpose and the political effect of section 2(c) is "nothing." Noble in concept but worthless in execution. He cannot get around the fact that the managers' report of both houses said as much when it said that subsequent sections of the joint resolution are not dependent on the language of section 2(c). The managers went so far as to say, "We want to show you this is not the Senate bill." So they took that out. . . . What we have here today is a 60- to 90-day open-ended blank check which says, "You fight the war for whatever reason, wherever you want to, Mr. President." That is what we are legislating here today.

The conference bill passed the Senate, 75–20. Few senators were in the chamber to hear the full debate; some, I later learned, assumed that the original Senate bill was fundamentally intact. The comments of senator after senator were directed at the original Senate bill rather than the conference bill. The change made by the conference committee seemed minor to most, a technicality, not important enough to change long-held positions. But without a legally binding delineation of authority, "the essence of meaningful war powers legislation," in Senator Javits' words, had been sacrificed. The President's claim of inherent power to initiate war would be given the color of legality.

On October 12, the House passed the conference bill by a vote of 238–123 and the war powers resolution went to the President for the expected veto.* A number of congressmen repeated arguments similar to mine before voting against the bill. But of the approximately thirty members previously opposed to the Indochina War who voted against the original House bill, only half opposed the new bill. Were the changed votes the result of satisfaction with the conference bill? Or did they reflect a growing resolve to defeat Richard Nixon on something?

On Saturday, October 20, the President's political stock hit a new low. After refusing for months to provide the grand jury investigating the Watergate matter with tape recordings of his conversations with key figures in the affair, he devised a plan to have Senator Stennis review the tapes personally and endorse a summary which would be given to the Court. When Archibald Cox, a former Harvard law professor of mine who had been appointed as special prosecutor in the case, learned he would have to cease his pursuit of the tapes and other key documents, he publicly announced his refusal to accept the President's compromise. That Saturday night the President asked Attorney General Elliott Richardson to fire Cox. Richardson resigned instead. When Deputy Attorney General William Ruckelshaus refused to fire Cox, he was fired. Solicitor General Robert Bork then fired Cox and the "Saturday-night massacre" was over. But in the weeks ahead the demand for impeachment

---

* The White House had long before publicly announced that the President would veto either the House or Senate bill.

came from all corners of the country and the House Judiciary Committee began to seriously consider the question. There were fewer and fewer congressmen who wanted to be identified as supporting the President, especially on a separation of powers dispute.

The anger and dismay over the precipitous firing of Special Prosecutor Cox had not yet subsided on October 25, when President Nixon vetoed the war powers resolution. Calling H. J. Res. 542 unconstitutional, he charged that it would "seriously undermine this Nation's ability to act decisively and convincingly in times of international crisis." There was nothing new in the message. The President was accustomed to operating in an extraconstitutional fashion, and any apparent restriction of his warmaking powers, even though his broad claim to initiate war was left untouched, was unacceptable. It didn't seem to matter that the bill would not stop the President from beginning a war single-handedly. That generous grant of authority would be acknowledged later, but now the President was complaining about an attempt to tie his hands ninety days after committing American forces to battle.

House advocates of the war powers resolution put on a major drive to secure the votes of those few dissident doves who had voted against the conference bill. A two-thirds majority was needed to override the veto. The pressure was on to defeat Richard Nixon and, ironically, the key swing votes were the President's most dedicated opponents. *The New Republic* and the *St. Louis Post Dispatch* opposed the conference bill, but most other national publications supported it editorially. The political forces were pulling strongly to override the veto. The rather dry legal arguments put forth were not making much headway. The President had vetoed eight bills in the Ninety-third Congress and eight times Congress failed to override him. It was an embarrassing record for the Democratic leadership, which was under fire in the media. The war powers vote would be its best chance yet to begin to even the score.

The override vote in the House took place on November 7. *Newsweek* magazine called it a tense scene with high-pressure lobbying carried on by both sides. The President himself called a number of key congressmen. The leadership leaned on those Democrats who claimed that the bill extended the President's powers. "This is no time to support Nixon," they said. Only seconds before the final tally a small group of liberals switched their votes in favor of the override. The final vote was 284–135. The House overrode the veto by four votes. One of the liberals who reluctantly switched her previous vote was Congresswoman Bella Abzug. She reflected the attitude of many:

> Until today, Congress has not been able to override any Presidential veto in this session. But today's vote comes at a time of revulsion of the people against the crimes and corruption in this administration. . . . This could be a turning point in the struggle to control an administration that has run amuck. It could accelerate the demand for the impeachment of the President.

The bill then came immediately before the Senate and I went to the chamber to urge my colleagues to reject it. As I came onto the floor, a respected senior senator called me aside and said, "Tom, we wish you would keep quiet on this vote. We simply have to

slap Nixon down and this is the vote to do it on." I
said that I could not keep quiet about a bill that gave
the President more power than the Constitution be-
stowed upon him. It was, to say the least, an awkward confrontation.

I glanced toward the press gallery and began my
speech: ". . . the media coverage of the bill still says
that [it] limits the President's war powers. It does
not. The bill gives the President unilateral authority
to commit American troops anywhere in the world,
under any conditions he decides, for 60 to 90
days. . . ."

Many senators understood this, but thought that
the provisions allowing Congress to stop a war by a
majority vote were worth the sacrifice. I again tried to
make the point that Congress had been conspicu-
ously reluctant to stop the President after American
forces were committed to battle. I related a 1969 conversation with the late Senator Richard Russell of
Georgia:

> In one of the early days after I had come to the
> Senate, I was seated, having lunch, in the little dining
> room where Senators sometimes dine. I was so new
> that I sat at the head of the table by mistake. I sat in
> the chair that, by custom, was reserved for the late
> Senator Richard Russell, of Georgia. No one told me
> to the contrary. Senator Russell came in to eat. He
> took another chair, he being the very fine gentleman
> that he was. Finally, somebody winked at me and told
> me I was in the wrong place. So I traded chairs, but I
> sat next to Senator Russell.
>
> Somewhere in the conversation, the discussion
> turned to war, how we get into it, and how hard it is to
> get out of it. It perhaps is not very well known, but

Senator Russell had personal misgivings in the sense of why we were there and what national security interests were being served by our massive presence there.

But he said:

> Whatever misgivings I had about that war—and I counseled with President Eisenhower about it in the early days; I counseled with President Kennedy about it; and I counseled with President Johnson about it—whatever misgivings I had, whatever doubts I had, so long as our flag is committed and our troops have been sent, I have got to support those troops and I have to support the flag when the decision is made.

That was what Senator Russell told me. He was a very wise man, one of the wisest ever to serve in this body. Those words of his are better than any that I could summon. Once the commitment has been made the die is cast.

Javits and Muskie seemed more intent on demonstrating that the bill would not overly restrict unilateral presidential action than on what it would do to Congress' role. They sent a "Dear Colleague" letter to all senators, which had been printed in the *Congressional Record* the day before. The letter referred to an October 6 outbreak of fighting in the Middle East. When a temporary cease-fire between Israeli and Arab forces broke down, the Soviet Union threatened to send ground forces to reimpose it. President Nixon reacted with a worldwide alert bringing our military forces to the brink of war. He never did commit them to battle, but the near-confrontation was an apt backdrop for the war powers debate. In their letter, Javits and Muskie used this situation to show how the war powers bill would work:

Nothing in the war powers resolution could have hampered the President in his handling of the recent Middle East crisis. The bill would have allowed the President to put our armed forces on alert, to order movements of our fleets and to resupply the Israelis with military equipment. *The bill would have required the President only to report to the Congress within 48 hours with respect to the deployment of U.S. Armed Forces in foreign territory, airspace and waters.* (Emphasis added.)

Senator Javits, who had earlier argued that the bill would not permit the President to introduce forces into battle without prior congressional consent, appeared in the letter to contradict himself. He explained the contradiction this way: ". . . nothing in the war powers resolution could have hampered the President in his handling of the recent Middle East crisis. . . . Of course, if he had introduced our forces further than he did . . . the bill would have and should have been operative."

Nevertheless, the important question remained: How would the bill operate? What would the President be required to do under its provisions? Javits contended that the President would be circumscribed by the knowledge that Congress could step in and stop him within ninety days. He would have to "take his chances" if his action was not legally correct, Javits argued. I addressed this contention in my summary argument:

If this becomes law we have given a predated declaration of war to the President and any other President of the United States, courtesy of the U.S. Congress. This is not a question of the President taking his chances. The chances he will be taking are our chances, our country's chances, chances with life and death.

What the President should do, in the mind of the Senator from New York, is to come to Congress. What does the bill provide? I served at one time in the Missouri Legislature. We had a member of the house there at one time get up and say, "I see what the bill say, but what do it do?" What does this bill do?

Section 2(c) is nonoperative and nonenforceable, not only by its policy section but by the very interpretation in the managers' report which was signed by the chief sponsors of the legislation, the Senator from Maine (MR. MUSKIE) and the Senator from New York (MR. JAVITS). They said in that report very clearly what section 2(c) did not do. It is here on page 8 of the manager's report.

The chance the Senator from New York is willing to have the President take is the chance to deploy our forces to a hostile area. And the President, under this measure, could deploy those troops in Israel, Syria, Egypt, Chile, Bangladesh, or wherever he wanted, tomorrow. There is a 60-day period but the troops are there. They are deployed, being shot at, dying, and the flag is committed. . . .

That is not what the Constitution of the United States envisaged when we were given the authority to declare war. We were to decide ab initio, at the outset, and not post facto.

This is no historic moment of circumscribing the President of the United States insofar as warmaking is concerned. This is an historic tragedy. It gives to the President and all of his successors in futuro, a pre-dated 60-day unilateral warmaking authority. All the words spoken here today cannot change what this law does, and what it does is wrong.

But the train had already left the station, powered by the notion that an override would be a rebuke of the President. One senator came up to me after the debate and said, "I heard your argument. I agree with you. I love the Constitution, but I hate Nixon more." Another said, "You were right as a matter of policy. But what you failed to recognize was that this had become a symbolic issue insofar as the public's perception of limiting the President's warmaking."

So the President was defeated, symbolically, 75–18. Sam Ervin and Jim Abourezk, who both opposed efforts to legislate in the war powers area, were the only other Democrats to vote with me to sustain the veto. Congress had answered the President's usurpation of its most solemn power by legitimizing it. The enactment of the war powers bill was the culmination of an era of congressional surrender.

On November 9, I wrote to Secretary of State Henry Kissinger and asked him for the State Department's legal interpretation of the newly enacted law. The debate over the meaning of the legislation was a tangle of contradictory assertions. The only practical way to expose the real effect of the bill, short of actually going to war, was to ask how the executive branch would implement its provisions. Would the President feel legally constrained by the definition of his emergency authority contained in the "Purpose and Policy" section of the bill?

The answer came prematurely and unexpectedly in an Associated Press bulletin reporting the comments of Secretary of Defense James Schlesinger at a November 30 press conference. I read the bulletin as it came over the wire service ticker near the Senate floor:

Washington (AP)—Defense Secretary James Schlesinger said today war powers legislation passed by the

Congress may make it possible for President Nixon to order new bombing in Indochina in the event of a new major North Vietnamese offensive in South Vietnam.

Though indicating he would likely oppose the idea, Schlesinger said the State Department is examining such a possibility.

The war powers legislation he referred to would give Nixon the authority to send U.S. forces into combat abroad for sixty days before Congressional authorization had to be obtained.

The bill became law over President Nixon's veto earlier this month.

It was now plain that the administration was reading the War Powers Resolution for what it was, an undated declaration of war. It was an unconstitutional delegation of congressional war powers, but in the context of continuing usurpations of these powers, the President would be the last to protect Congress from its own legislative formula. The ninety-day grant of authority would apparently be taken at face value, to be used to augment the increasingly discredited presidential claims to initiate war unilaterally.

The War Powers Resolution was a blank check to be used as legal tender for claims of inherent executive power, but according to its provisions it could not be used as "specific authorization." It could not, therefore, be used to supersede the Church-Case provision in the State Department authorization bill stating that no funds may be expended for combat activity in Indochina "unless specifically authorized hereafter by Congress." Secretary Kissinger publicly conceded this point the following week, but by then it was quite clear how the administration would implement the War Powers Resolution in areas of the world where specific restrictions did not apply.

On December 1, I received the State Department's response to my request for a legal interpretation. "It is the Department's opinion that Section 2(c) does not constitute a legally binding definition of the President's Constitutional power as Commander-in-Chief," the letter stated. "Section 2 does not contain language which requires or prohibits any particular action. . . ." The department was still studying the implications of the operative sections of the bill (calling for consultation, reporting, and congressional authorization to continue a war beyond ninety days), but whether or not the President decided he would abide by those legally binding sections or challenge them as unconstitutional, his State Department clearly saw the bill as a ninety-day open-ended grant of authority.

How did it happen? How could Congress formalize its surrender to executive power in the warmaking area in the immediate aftermath of a tragic presidential war? I have given that paradox considerable thought but have no final answer. Had Congress lost confidence in the Constitution and the institutional mechanisms created by that document? There is a pervasive feeling that principles espoused by the founders simply don't apply to the modern age. The *New York Times* reflected this attitude in its November 8 editorial acclaiming the enactment of the War Powers Resolution:

> The war powers bill itself is not the revolutionary measure that Mr. Nixon and other critics have attempted to make it out to be. It does not in any way curtail the President's freedom, as Commander in

Chief, to respond to emergency situations. *If any-thing, it gives the Chief Executive more discretionary authority than the framers of the Constitution intended in order to deal with modern contingencies that they could not have foreseen.*

Life has changed since the time of the founders, but the necessity for deliberation and collective judgment is, if anything, more important today. In 1787, the most likely threat to the United States was the British fleet storming the east coast. In the 1970s the American military presence is everywhere. War could break out involving any of the more than two thousand military installations overseas, and war could begin with the push of a button. We continue to require a commander in chief who can act expeditiously to "repel sudden attacks," but we require more than ever a responsible Congress to decide when national "interests" and "commitments" should lead to war. If the experience of Vietnam has taught us anything, it should have taught that the choice between war and peace is best left to the collective judgment of Congress and the President. There is no guarantee of perfection in such a system, but it is infinitely safer than one man acting alone. The admonition of Supreme Court Justice Joseph Story in 1833, is still relevant today:

> The power of declaring war is not only the highest sovereign prerogative; but it is in its own nature and effects so critical and calamitous, that it requires the utmost deliberation, and the successive review of all the councils of the nation.

Implicit in the argument that Congress cannot perform its function of declaring war in the modern world is the frustration over Congress' inability to step in and take over for a weak President in other areas. Congress is comprised of 535 members. It can never be as dynamic and decisive as the one man to whom the great powers of the presidency are assigned. But the founders understood that the line between dynamism and arrogance, between decisiveness and tyranny, is a precariously thin one. They purposely devised a deliberate, diverse, and accessible body that would subject the most important questions facing us to the scrutiny of collective judgment. Much can be done to improve the process of deliberation, but progress will be slow if Congress misunderstands its own fundamental role.

The primary responsibility of the legislature in this instance is to declare war, not stop it after it has begun. Congress is at a distinct disadvantage in trying to terminate a conflict over the objections of the commander in chief.

The founders could not have anticipated the contingencies of a modern America, but they were studied in the arrogance of excessive power and they knew well how to limit it. I suspect that if Hamilton and Madison and Jefferson could be brought back to view contemporary America, they would be less alarmed by the modern tools of mass destruction than by the erosion of the constitutional means they created to control their use.

Many have grown cynical over the failure of Congress to curb presidential power. If this book feeds that cynicism, its message has been missed. I labored to enact war powers legislation, because I believed that the intent of the Constitution could be recaptured by statute. It can still be done, but it will require a wider conviction that the system can work.

It will require faith in law over the transitory desires of politicians. And it will require a keener awareness by the public that the most important decision a free society makes is the decision to go or not to go to war.

Bibliography

Austin, Anthony. *The President's War*. Philadelphia: J. B. Lippincott Co., 1971.

Barnet, Richard J. *Roots of War*. New York: Atheneum Publishers, 1971.

Bickel, Alexander M. "The Constitution and the War." *Commentary* 54 (July 1972) : 49–55.

Bickel, Alexander *and others*. "Indochina: The Constitutional Crisis." *Congressional Record* (daily ed.) 116 (May 13, 1970) : s7117–s7123. Part II, *Congressional Record* (daily ed.) 116 (May 20, 1970) : s7538–s7531.

Burns, James MacGreger. *The Deadlock of Democracy*. Englewood Cliffs, N.J.: Prentice-Hall Inc., 1963.

———. *Presidential Government: The Crucible of Leadership*. Boston: Houghton Mifflin, 1966.

Commager, Henry Steele. *The Defeat of America*. New York: Simon and Schuster, Inc., 1974.

"Congress, the President, and the Power to Commit Forces to Combat." Note, *Harvard Law Review* 81 (June 1968) : 1771–1805.

Collidge, Francis L., Jr., Sharrow, Joel David. *The War-making Powers: the Intentions of the Framers in Light of Parliamentary History*. *Boston University Law Review* 50 (1970) : 4–18.

Dahl, Robert. *Congress and Foreign Policy*. New York: Harcourt, Brace and Company, 1950.

Dverin, Eugene, ed. *The Senate's War Powers; Debate on Cambodia from the Congressional Record.* Chicago: Markham Publishing Co., 1971.

Eagleton, Thomas F. "Congress and War Powers." *Missouri Law Review* 37 (Winter 1972) : 1–32.

———. "Whose Power Is War Power?" *Foreign Policy* 8 (Fall 1972) : 23–32.

———. "The August 15 Compromise and the War Powers of Congress." *St. Louis University Law Journal* 18 (Fall 1973) : 1–11.

Emerson, J. T. "War Powers Legislation." *West Virginia Law Review* 74 (November–January, 1971–1972) : 53–119.

Faulkner, S. "War in Vietnam: Is It Constitutional?" *Georgetown Law Journal* 56 (June 1968) : 1132–1143.

Fulbright, J. William. *The Arrogance of Power.* New York: Random House, 1967.

———. "Congress, the President and the War Powers." *Arkansas Law Review* 25 (Spring 1971) : 71–84.

Goldman, Eric F. "The President, the People and the Power to Make War." *American Heritage* 21 (April 1970) : 4–35.

Goldwater, Barry M. "President's Ability to Protect America's Freedoms—the Warmaking Power." *Law and Social Order* 1971 no. 2 : 423–449.

Halberstam, David. *The Best and the Brightest.* New York: Random House, 1972.

Henkin, Louis. "Viet-Nam in the Courts of the United States: 'Political Questions.' " *American Journal of International Law* 63 (April 1969) : 284–289.

Hilsman, Roger. *To Move a Nation; The Politics of Foreign Policy in the Administration of John F. Kennedy.* Garden City, New York: Doubleday, 1967.

Hughes, Emmet J. *The Living Presidency.* New York: Coward, McCann & Geoghegan, 1973.

Javits, Jacob K. "Congress and the President; a Modern Delineation of the War Powers." *Albany Law Review* 35 no. 4 (1971) : 632–637.

———. *Who Makes War.* New York: William Morrow and Company, Inc., 1973.

Katzenbach, Nicholas. "Comparative Roles of the President and the Congress in Foreign Affairs." *The Department of State Bulletin* 47 (September 11, 1967) : 333–336.

————. "Congress and Foreign Policy." *Cornell International Law Journal* 3 (Winter 1970) : 33.

Keewn, Stuart S. "The President, the Congress, and the Power to Declare War." *University of Kansas Law Review* 16 (November 1967) : 82–97.

Lefgren, Charles A. "War-making Under the Constitution: The Original Understanding." *Yale Law Journal* 81 (March 1972) : 672–702.

MacIver, Kenneth F., Jr.; Wolff, Beverly M.; and Lecke, Leonard Bruch. "The Supreme Court as Arbitrator in the Conflict Between Presidential and Congressional War-making Powers." *Boston University Law Review* 50 (1970) : 78–116.

Malawer, Stuart S. "The Vietnam War Under the Constitution: Legal Issues Involved in the United States Military Involvement in Vietnam." *University of Pittsburgh Law Review* 31 (Winter 1969) : 205–241.

May, Ernest. *The Ultimate Decision: the President as Commander in Chief.* New York: George Braziller Inc., 1960.

Meeker, Leonard C. "The Legality of United States Participation in the Defense of Viet-Nam." *Department of State Bulletin* 54 (April 28, 1966) : 474–489.

Mikva, Abner J. and Joseph R. Lundy. "The 91st Congress and the Constitution." *University of Chicago Law Review* 38 (Spring 1971) : 449–499.

Monaghan, Henry P. "Presidential war-making." *Boston University Law Review* 50 (1970) : 19–33.

Moore, John Norton. "Legal Dimensions of the Decision to Intercede in Cambodia." *American Journal of International Law* 65 (January 1971) : 38–75.

————. "The National Executive and the Use of Armed Forces Abroad." *In* Richard A. Falk, *ed. The Vietnam War and International Law.* American Society of International Law. Princeton, New Jersey: Princeton University Press, 1969.

Moore, John Norton; Underwood, James L.; and McDougal, Myres S. "The Lawfulness of United States Assistance to the Republic of Vietnam." *Congressional Record* 112 part 12 (July 13, 1966) : 15519–15567.

Neustadt, Richard E. *Presidential Power, the Politics of Leadership.* New York: Wiley and Sons, 1960.

Notes. "Congress, the President, and the Power to Commit Forces to Combat." *Harvard Law Review* 81 no. 8 (June 1968) · 1771–1805.

Pelsby, Nelson W. *Congress and the Presidency*. Englewood Cliffs, N.J.: Prentice-Hall Inc., 1964.

Pusey, Merlo J. "The President and the Power to Make War." *Atlantic Monthly* (July 1969) : 65–67.

———. *The Way We Go to War*. Boston: Houghton Mifflin Company, 1969.

Rehnquist, William H. "The Constitutional Issues—Administration Position." *New York University Law Review* 45 (June 1970) : 628–639.

Reveley, W. Taylor, III. "Presidential Warmaking: Constitutional Prerogative or Usurpation?" *Virginia Law Review* 55 (November 1969) : 1243–1305.

Rogers, William P. "Congress, the President, and the War Powers." *California Law Review* 59 (September 1971) : 1194–1214.

Rogers, William D. "The Constitutionality of the Cambodian Incursion." *American Journal of International Law* 65 (January 1971) : 26–37.

Rossiter, Clinton L. *The American Presidency*. New York: Harcourt Brace Jovanovich, 1963.

Rostow, Eugene V. "Great Cases Make Bad Law: The War Powers Act." *Texas Law Review* 50 (May 1972) : 833–900.

Schlesinger, Arthur, Jr. "Congress and the Making of American Foreign Policy." *Foreign Affairs* 51 (Oct. 1972) : 78–113.

———. *The Imperial Presidency*. Boston: Houghton Mifflin Company, 1973.

———. "The limits and excesses of Presidential power." *Saturday Review* 52 (May 3, 1969) : 17–19.

Scribner, Jeffrey L. "The President Versus Congress on War Making Authority." *Military Review* 52 (April 1972) : 87–96.

Spong, W. B., Jr. "Can Balance Be Restored in the Constitutional War Powers of the President and Congress?" *University of Richmond Law Review* 6 (Fall 1971) : 1–47.

Symposium of lawyers on Indochina, May 20, 1970. *Congressional Record* (daily ed.), 116, May 28, 1970 : s7967–s7975. (Legal participants were Francis Plimpton, George Lindsay, Adrian Dewind, Robert McKay, Alexander Bickel, and Abram Chayes.)

Tigar, Michael E. "Judicial Power, the 'Political Question Doctrine,' and Foreign Relations." *UCLA Law Review* 17 (June 1970) : 1135–1179.

Tugwell, Rexford G. *The Enlargement of the Presidency.* New York: Doubleday and Company, 1960.

U.S. Congress, House, Committee on Foreign Affairs, *Report . . . Pursuant to H. Res. 28.* 82nd Congress, 1st session, February 20, 1951, H. Rept. 127.

U.S. Congress, House, Committee on Foreign Affairs, Subcommittee on National Security Policy and Scientific Developments, *War Powers Legislation: Hearings,* 93rd Congress, 1st sess. March 7, 8, 13, 14, 15, 20, 1973.

———. *Concerning the War Powers of Congress and the President: Report to Accompany H. J. Res. 1.,* 92nd Cong., 2nd sess., 1971, H. Rept. 91–1547.

———. *Concerning the War Powers of Congress and the President: Report to Accompany H. J. Res. 1355,* 91st Cong., 2nd sess., 1970, H. Rept. 91–1547.

———. *Concerning the War Powers of Congress and the President: Report to Accompany S. 2956,* 92d Cong., 2nd sess., 1972, H. Rept. 92–1302.

———. *Background Information on the Use of United States Armed Forces in Foreign Countries* (1970 revision by the Foreign Affairs Division, Legislative Reference Service, Library of Congress.), 91st Congress, 2nd sess., 1970.

———. *War Powers Legislation: Hearings,* 92nd Cong., 1st sess., June 1 and 2, 1971.

U.S. Congress, Senate, Committee on Foreign Relations, *Amending the Foreign Military Sales Act: Report to Accompany H. R. 15628,* 91st Congress, 2nd session, May 12, 1970.

———. *War Powers Legislation: Hearings,* 93rd Congress, 1st sess., April 11 and 12, 1973.

———. *Background information on the Committee on Foreign Relations, United States Senate. Rev. ed.,* 90th Congress, 2nd sess., 1968.

———. *Documents Relating to the War Power of Congress, the President's Authority as Commander-in-Chief and the War in Indochina,* 91st Cong., 2nd sess., 1970.

————. *Foreign Military Sales Act Amendment; 1970: Hearing on S. 2640, S. 3429 and H.R. 15628,* 91st Congress, 2nd sess., March 24 and May 11, 1970.

————. *National Commitments: Report to Accompany S. Res. 187,* 90th Congress, 1st sess., 1967.

————. *National Commitments: Report, Together with Minority Views to Accompany S. Res. 85,* 91st Congress, 1st sess., April 16, 1969.

————. *Termination of Southeast Asia Resolution: Report to Accompany S. Con. Res. 64,* 91st Congress, 2nd sess., May 15, 1070.

————. *U.S. Commitments to Foreign Powers: Hearings on S. Res. 151,* 90th Congress, 1st sess., August 16, 17, 21, 23 and September 19, 1967.

————. *Vietnam Policy Proposals: Hearings,* 91st Congress, 2nd sess., February 3, 4, 5, and March 16, 1970.

————. *War Powers Legislation: Hearings on S. 731, S.J. Res. 18 and S.J. Res. 59,* 92nd Congress, 1st sess., 1972.

————. *War Powers: Report Together with Additional Views of Senator Fulbright and Individual Views of Senator John Sherman Cooper, to Accompany S. 2956,* 92nd Cong., 2nd sess., 1972.

U.S. Congress, Senate, Committee on Foreign Relations and Committee on Armed Services, *Powers of the President to Send the Armed Forces Outside the United States,* 82nd Congress, 1st sess., February 28, 1951.

U.S. Congress, Senate, Committee on the Judiciary, Subcommittee on Separation of Powers, *Hearings,* 90th Congress, 1st sess., July 19 and 20; August 2; and September 13 and 15, 1967.

U.S. Congress, House Resolved: that Executive control of United States foreign policy should be significantly curtailed. A collection of excerpts and bibliography relating to the national collegiate debate topic, 1968–69. 90th Congress, 2nd session (House Document 298). Washington, U.S. Govt. Print. Off., 1968. 266 pp.

Velvel, Lawrence R. "The War in Viet Nam: Unconstitutional, Justiciable and Jurisdictionally Attackable." *Kansas Law Review* 16 (1968) : 449.

Weeters, Garry J. "The Appropriations Power as a Tool of Congressional Foreign Policy Making." *Boston University Law Review* 50 (1970) : 34–50.

Wormuth, Francis D. "The Nixon Theory of the War Power: A Critique." *California Law Review* 60 (May 1972).

Wright, Quincy. "The power of the executive to use military forces abroad." *Virginia Journal of International Law* 10 (December 1969) : 42–57.

Index

ABOUT THE AUTHOR

Thomas F. Eagleton is U.S. Senator (Democrat) from Missouri. He was born in St. Louis in 1929 and is a graduate of Amherst College and the Harvard Law School. After being the youngest Circuit (District) Attorney in the history of St. Louis, the youngest Attorney General of Missouri, and Lieutenant Governor of Missouri, he was elected to the Senate in 1968. Since then he has become one of the leading advocates for restoring the Constitutional balance between Congress and the Executive branch. *War and Presidential Power* is his first book.

DATE DUE